The New Library Legacy:

Essays in Honor
of Richard De Gennaro

Susan A. Lee (Editor)

K·G·Saur München 1998

Die Deutsche Bibliothek – CIP-Einheitsaufnahme

The new library legacy : essays in honor of Richard DeGennaro /
Susan A. Lee, ed. – München : Saur, 1998
ISBN 3-598-11389-7

Printed on acid-free paper

© 1998 by K. G. Saur Verlag GmbH & Co. KG, München
Part of Reed Elsevier
Printed in the Federal Republic of Germany

Printed by Strauss Offsetdruck, Mörlenbach
Bound by Buchbinderei Schaumann, Darmstadt

ISBN 3-598-11389-7

Table of Contents

Table of Contents

Foreword

by Cheryl LaGuardia
Coordinator of Electronic Teaching Center
Harvard College Library

When I arrived at Harvard in late 1994, I stood outside Richard De Gennaro's office in Widener Library waiting trepidaciously to meet him: I seldom get the opportunity to meet library legends in the flesh. As I stood there I remembered an article by De Gennaro in *Library Journal* that I had read in graduate school at a point when I was questioning my choice of profession. I'd been wading that day through a lot of gobbledygook library automation writing (a la the programmer's perspective), but when I read this article, its clarity and intelligence convinced me that perhaps librarianship was a reasonable profession after all.

More than anything else, I was struck by the author's sheer common sense, his rational approach to a complex issue, and the easily-accessible way in which he laid out his arguments. Richard De Gennaro. Hmmm. I liked the way the man's mind worked. I followed his work with interest after that, and when the opportunity came for me to write a monthly column for *Library Journal*, I tried to follow the examples I'd learned from De Gennaro's many writings: keep to the issues and keep your message clear and accessible.

Now I was waiting to meet the man himself. The office door opened, and a pleasantly smiling face greeted me warmly, took me by the hand, and said, "I read your column all the time, and I'm a big fan. I'm so glad finally to meet you." The legend was, in fact, a very charming gentleman who went out of his way to put me at my ease, who complimented me on my work and began to talk about what I could do for Harvard and what Harvard could do for me.

I count myself extraordinarily fortunate to have been able to work with Richard De Gennaro during the last two years of his career at Harvard. His groundbreaking work with library technology and his ability to communicate the need to embrace new technologies helped define and shape new libraries as we are coming to know them: a combination of printed text, images, data, photographs, videos, music, ephemera, and artwork available in a rich array of formats and avenues of access. Dick's common sense approach to innovation will influence the very nature of research libraries well into the 21st century and beyond.

Dedication

by Susan A. Lee
Associate Librarian of Harvard College for Administrative Services

One of the universal cravings of our time is an abiding hunger for compelling and creative leadership. This is perhaps felt even more in libraries than in the rest of our society. This publication honors one who has joined the pantheon of library leaders -- one of the true giants to stride across our intellectual and professional landscape. Richard De Gennaro's vision, combined with his unswerving conviction about the research library's social mission and the essential role it plays in a democratic society, have defined his lengthy distinguished career. De Gennaro has devoted a professional lifetime to research library management. The qualities of his character -- his drive, his dedication, and perhaps most important, his tenacity -- embody the definition of a true Statesman-leader.

Throughout his career, De Gennaro has been well known as an innovator. He is a man of great ideas and major objectives, a person who has motivated, activated, and mobilized all those around him. He has been an inspiration, both to those of us who have worked with him and to the profession at large. He raised our expectations for ourselves, inducing us to act for goals that represent the highest aspirations of professional achievement. At the same time, he has never lost sight -- nor let us lose sight -- of the practical, substantial side of our profession and our work. As new problems and issues have challenged the profession, De Gennaro's ability to reshape opinion and realign support for new ideas and programs on a grand scale has been unmatched.

All leaders must be able to inspire a shared vision and set common goals. Throughout his career, De Gennaro has showed us that doing so is about personal character, not charades. He is a man of substance, not symbolism -- a man with soul as well as style. The research library community, and especially we, his colleagues here at Harvard, are the richer for having rubbed shoulders with this "living legend" (Dick has always insisted on using quotation marks on this phrase -- we would leave them off).

While this book is a tribute to a distinguished career, these papers also reflect their own intrinsic quality and value. For those who are concerned about the future of our research libraries they are valuable contributions from a group of Dick's close friends and noteworthy thinkers in the field.

The final measure of a leader is the record of accomplishment they leave behind, the degree of "real change" they bring to the lives of others and the improvements they ultimately leave for the profession. Judged by this standard of actual accomplishment for promised change, Richard De Gennaro is very special indeed.

Acknowledgments

I owe a great debt to the many people whose extraordinary efforts contributed to the success of this volume. My warmest thanks to all those who without a moment's pause, enthusiastically endorsed and contributed to this effort to honor and build on the work of Richard De Gennaro. Special appreciation is expressed to:

Carol Ishimoto for the initial idea of this collection and for the compilation of essential materials;
Sue Martin for her early assistance in identifying our list of contributors;
Cheryl LaGuardia for her ongoing constructive criticisms, insightful comments and valuable suggestions;
This distinguished group of Dick's colleagues for sharing their current perspectives and assessing so eloquently their view of the potential developments of the next decade.

We are grateful also for help so generously given by Elizabeth Johnson and Kate Eckhaus -- model proof readers, coordinators and organizers. Their careful attention to detail throughout the project increased the quality of the product and their infinite flexibility and humor kept us all sanely on course.

Susan A. Lee
Cambridge, Massachusetts

Preface

by Neil L. Rudenstine
President, Harvard University

Richard De Gennaro has long been a preeminent presence in the world of the research library. *Vision* is a word we tend to overuse—but Dick De Gennaro has long possessed a compelling vision, and he has pursued it over the course of decades, with deeply impressive results. He has been at the forefront of redefining the role of the library through an era of explosive growth in information and dramatic changes in technology. He has conceived of the library as a living organism—in constant need of nourishment, adaptation, and care, so that each of its many parts can contribute effectively to the creation of a vital whole. He has always looked forward: anticipating significant trends, planning for new needs, and combining the highest academic aspirations with an uncommon capacity to get things done.

I have been seriously disappointed with Dick only once in the nearly twenty years since we first met. That was when he concluded, in 1979, that he was unable to leave his responsibilities at the University of Pennsylvania in order to become the librarian at Princeton, despite my own and others' efforts to lure him there. Fortunately, I have had my longstanding hope ultimately realized, in a totally unanticipated way: when I returned to Harvard in 1991, I discovered to my delight that Dick had recently been appointed as Librarian of Harvard College. It has been an undiluted pleasure to work with him ever since.

Our research libraries are obviously experiencing a period of fundamental and rapid change. Knowledge and information continue to grow at an often breathtaking pace. The costs of acquiring new books and journals, and of storing and preserving existing materials, pose unusual difficulties for institutions determined to sustain the high quality of their collections while living within intensified budgetary constraints. And, perhaps most important, the rise of the Internet and associated technologies promises transformative changes that we are only beginning to experience and understand.

Insofar as we are well prepared to confront these challenges—and to make the most of the opportunities that accompany them — our readiness is due in no small part to the imagination, foresight, and hard work of Richard De Gennaro. All of us who care about libraries, and about excellent scholarship, owe him a profound debt of gratitude. I am privileged to introduce this collection prepared in his honor. And I am proud to join in thanking him for all he has done—and will continue to do—to make our research libraries ever stronger and ever new.

Introduction

Richard De Gennaro: An Appreciation

by Sidney Verba
Director, Harvard University Library

Libraries and Information

The United States has always been a nation dominated by the automobile. Henry Ford's assembly line factories shaped our industrial life; the automobiles he and others produced provided the mobility and autonomy that made America's working class into a middle class society; and the car shaped our cities, our suburbs, and our landscape. So we know that we are dealing with something important when we use an automobile based term -- the super-highway -- to talk about information.

The twentieth century is ending on an information high. We are in the midst of an information revolution. It is big business, and it is an important political issue. It is no accident that most large corporations have an information vice-president -- and so does the nation.

For libraries, the discovery of the centrality of information is not news. They have been in the information business for a long time. Libraries, furthermore, remind us of history and that this is not the first time new technologies have profoundly altered the flow of information. Other information revolutions -- from the invention of printing to the invention of cheap paper and high speed presses -- changed the dissemination of information and changed society. These earlier changes also affected libraries. There was a need for new technologies and new skills to deal with the volume of new information. Libraries responded with shelving systems and catalogues; appropriate mechanisms for storing and finding the information.

Change is not new, but the pace of change in information technology is certainly greater now than ever before. The biggest change -- certainly the latest and most dramatic -- has been the introduction of digital technology to information. Digital technology changes the library world. Traditional libraries were based on information-laden objects -- mostly books and journals -- in specific physical locations. The job of the library and the librarian was to select the objects worth keeping, arrange them in some logical order so that they could be found, provide finding aids such as catalogues to locate them, protect them, and make them available to users who show up to read them. Digital information, in contrast to information on paper, is not bound by location, and it is not locked into physical objects. It can be manipulated and copied; it can be sent elsewhere and still remain where it is.

The change has had a great effect and will have an even greater effect in the future on libraries. But the effect will not be what some have anticipated: the demise of the book, of the library, and of the librarian. We will still need all three. Books and journals remain the dominant modes of production for information; indeed, they are a mode of production that produces more each year. Someday this may change but probably not in the near to mid-term future. However, the way in which books and journals are stored, located, and used is being affected by digital technology. Some journals, and a few books, are in digital form. But all books and journals are recorded and located using digital catalogues. And many may be shared through digital means. Nevertheless, paper remains at the heart of scholarship, and is still the predominant means of scholarly production. And that means libraries and librarians.

Libraries and librarians are needed not just because we still collect and provide paper resources. The functions they provide in relation to paper are needed in relation to digital information. In the world of paper, librarians do more than collect books and journals. They select what to collect from a much larger universe; they put it into some rational order; they certify and protect the authenticity of the materials; they help people find what they want; they deliver it in usable form; and they preserve and protect the materials into the future.

They do these things for books and journals, and these functions are even more vital when it comes to digital information. The volume of the material, its fragility, the fact that many producers and users want it now and do not care where it is tomorrow, the multiplicity of formats, the complexity of ownership, the technical issues associated with preservation, the uncertainty of who has responsibility for preservation: all these issues and more make it clear that those who talk of all the information in the Library of Congress being in a hat box are wrong. The new information is more a Pandora's box of new tasks and challenges.

At the heart of the enterprise, I believe, is the task of preserving and giving order to our history. Many institutions -- from newspapers and newsstands, to publishers and bookstores, to database producers and the Internet -- are in the business of delivering information to those who want and need it. But only the library worries about what happens to it after its current use. This is not an easy task and is more complex and difficult in the digital age.

There is money to be made in digital information, but it is usually to be made in current use. Today's world news or financial reports are valuable, and the production of such information is lucrative. So is the delivery. The company with a new delivery mechanism on the Internet can make millions with a stock offering. But history is, well, ...history. Thus, the great task of preserving our history and heritage -- the library's task -- is each year larger and each year less well funded.

Libraries are not often thought of as heroic institutions, and librarians are not considered heroes. Those appellations are reserved for institutions like the military and individuals who play basketball. But the work of libraries is heroic and, librarians who do more and more with less and less are heroes. Their heroism would only be noticed if they were not there -- if they had not performed their functions and, in later years, we wanted to trace our history.

This book contains a set of essays about the changing world of research libraries written by some of the heroes of the library world. They are the people who guided the libraries through some remarkable decades of change and adjustment. The authors of the essays have been directors of major libraries, heads of national library organizations, and publishers. Many have worn more than one hat. They have both made the library revolution and have been carried along with it. From the tone of their essays, it seems safe to say that none has been the victim of the revolution. The essays convey enthusiasm. They are not merely survivors of the revolution but people who look back with pride on what has been accomplished.

It is especially fitting that these essays appear in a Festschrift for Richard De Gennaro, one of the greatest of the heroes. As much as anyone, Dick De Gennaro has been at the center of the changes in research libraries. In his career in research libraries, he has wandered up and down the Northeast urban corridor, from New York to Cambridge to Philadelphia, back to New York, and then back to Cambridge. But his career has been much more wide ranging than that. He has been a leader in such national organizations as ARL and RLG and a mentor to librarians across the country. More than that, his leadership and vision have helped shape research libraries everywhere.

Some of the essays in this volume deal with the range of Dick's writings and his achievements. I want to focus on two aspects of his career: the De Gennaro style and the De Gennaro contribution to the Harvard Library.

The De Gennaro Style

The *Idealistic Realist (or the Realistic Idealist): Effective* change -- revolutionary change that works -- requires two kinds of people: visionaries to see beyond the current practices and procedures of an institution and realists who keep the visionaries from being carried away. Without the former, there can be no break from the past; without the latter, the break from the past can lead nowhere or, worse, can lead to disaster. Dick De Gennaro is one of those rare persons who combines both; who has been a "foot-on-the-ground visionary".

Dick saw, early on, the coming of the electronic revolution in libraries. As his writings show, he knew that it would change how libraries function and change them in profound ways. Libraries would have to adjust. Yet, he never signed on to the notion that libraries would become obsolete; that all knowledge would be loaded on one computer chip and carried around by each individual in a Walkman size virtual library. Dick knows hype when he sees it, and he recognized the hype -- which only gets louder each year -- early on. He knew that libraries would have to change; they could not wait for change to wash over them. But they also could not leap into the dark. They had to move forward firmly yet cautiously, as they still must do so.

There have been book people and byte people, those who saw the book as the core of the library and were satisfied that the core be the entire library and those who saw the book as an obsolete technology soon to be replaced by electronic information. The clearest visionaries saw that we would have both, in some uncertain but complex mixture. Dick was one of those clear visionaries.

Budgets: Nothing holds a visionary in check better than a budget. People who have to calculate the cost associated with a benefit cannot fly too high. And it is good that they face limitations, for the flight is likely to arrive somewhere. If anything could have kept Icarus from flying too close to the sun, it would have been a budget constraint -- and he would have been better off for it. Dick has always been a library manager -- at Penn., at New York Public, at Harvard. As such, he has had to be a realist. And that has helped him develop a vision that can, in fact, guide people as to what to do -- a vision circumscribed by reality. People who can combine the two are people whose advice one wants to take seriously -- because it is advice that can be put to use.

The combination of a budget constraints with the realization that libraries have to add bytes to the books -- with all the additional expenses that new technologies entail -- makes De Gennaro an advocate of new technologies as well as an advocate of the maintenance of traditional collections. And it makes him someone who knows how tough it is to do both.

Cooperation: De Gennaro was one of a small but influential group of librarians and foundation executives who realized early on that libraries had to work together if they were to continue to accomplish what they wanted to accomplish. The task was not easy. In the United States, massive tasks are rarely delegated to a single institution and so a proliferation of organizations were active on library cooperation: the Association of Research Libraries, the Research Libraries Group, OCLC, the Council on Library Resources; not to mention a variety of ad hoc groupings of two or more libraries. Dick was always in the midst of it all. As an idealist, he was dedicated to cooperation; as a realist, he knew it was hard to achieve and required (and requires) constant work.

Dick also knew (and knows) that cooperation takes a lot of committees and meetings -- one needs what the Germans call Sitzfleisch. Perhaps what makes Dick effective in these matters is that he has a lot, but not an unlimited amount, of Sitzfleisch. He can sit, talk, and negotiate with the best of them. But one of his favorite phrases is "let's just get on with it".

De Gennaro at Harvard

Dick chose to spend the last years of his library director career at Harvard, where he was the Roy E. Larsen Librarian of Harvard College. The Harvard College Library is, of course, not a college library but a great university library. It encompasses all the libraries of the Faculty of Arts and Sciences with Widener as the flagship. By itself -- without the professional school libraries which are under independent management -- it would still rank at the top of the ARL list.

He has left an indelible mark. He brought to the position all the aspects of the De Gennaro style. He has been an idealistic realist; he has helped move the Harvard College Library into the digital age while maintaining the commitment to the traditional book collection, and he has brought Harvard into the center of the national library community. He has sat through endless meetings and listened to many sides -- as one must do in any complex organization, especially at a university, and especially at a university as decentralized as is Harvard -- but has always at the end "got on with it".

The Harvard College Library was, when Dick arrived, a great library. Its greatness was in the collection. And its greatness was being maintained by a staff dedicated to careful and systematic collecting. But collecting was not enough. The College Library was faced with the multiplicity of problems facing all research libraries: the emerging digital technologies, a shortage of space, a collection sorely in need of preservation, a need to cooperate with other institutions to maximize the benefits of resource sharing.

The greatness of the collections made the problem more severe. Providing on-line access to one of the largest collections anywhere is daunting. Preservation is more difficult and more pressing when the collection is so vast and so valuable. And, above all, the obligation to keep collecting in order to fulfill the University's historical mission meant that these new demands would have to coexist with a continuation of more traditional tasks. It was a very large circle to square.

Dick began with a strategic plan -- or, rather, a strategic planning process. The process brought the various parts of the library together to consider the complex set of issues facing it. Out of the process came a renewed College Library. The plan was not a comprehensive redesign of everything. One cannot do that in a 350 year old institution, and one would not want to. Institutions that grow gradually have, as Edmund Burke taught us, a wisdom of their own. To pluck them out by the roots is the road to disaster. But institutions need a shaking once in a while, and Dick provided it.

Under his leadership, the College Library began an effective attack on the space problem. The Harvard Depository, which had opened shortly before his arrival, provided a location for the overflow of the books in Widener and the other College Libraries. The strategic plan developed a program of using it effectively -- essentially solving the space problem for the foreseeable future. Shortly after Dick's arrival, the College Library, along with the rest of the University Library system, began the largest retrospective conversion program ever undertaken, a program that will put into digital form all the records of the vast Harvard collection. Before his arrival, there were few electronic resources in the College Library; now it is hard to keep track of them. And on and on.

The Harvard Library may be likened to a super-tanker. Its cargo is of immense value; it has the size and power to deliver that cargo where it is needed. But once a super-tanker is underway, it takes a good deal of time and effort to change its direction. Dick De Gennaro has steered the Harvard College Library toward the 21st century. The seas will not always be smooth -- but the right course has been set.

Technology and the Humanities

by Patricia Battin

One of the painful results of the continuing utilization of information technology by research libraries has been the growing schism, and in some instances, downright hostility, between the formerly staunch allies who built the great research libraries of the world—humanists and librarians. As librarians began to use computer technology to manage their operations, replace card catalogs, and provide electronic information resources, humanists became greatly concerned that traditional priorities and expenditures for developing book collections were shifting to an undue emphasis on technologies that had yet to demonstrate any significant value to humanities scholarship. Indeed, many humanists believe that digital technology has essentially destroyed the culture of the book that has nourished the humanities for over 500 years.

Dick De Gennaro's career reflects this difficult period as he led his colleagues in three major research libraries to realize the potential of digital technology to enhance and expand scholarly inquiry and discovery in all disciplines. With the new frenzy over the predicted transformational powers of the Internet and a still-abstract concept called "the digital library," it is time to reaffirm our historic affiliation and use our respective perspectives and strengths to make sure the humanities will indeed flourish in the technological society.

An enduring—but not endearing—characteristic of our analog human minds seems to be the implacable conviction that each new invention will substitute rather than complement what already exists, that it will eliminate the competition rather than provide us with the opportunity for choices best suited to the task at hand.

It is certainly true that horses and buggies are hard to find these days except in Amish communities, that washtubs and elbow grease have been supplanted by computerized Maytags, and electric lighting has replaced the gaslamp. In each of these cases, I would argue that the capacity of the new invention proved overwhelmingly superior in performing the primary function of its forerunner. One can also point to other instances of "progress" where the rush to embrace the new has been less successful because we did not understand the more complex function of that which we were replacing with new technology. Two examples here are railroad transportation and tomatoes. In both instances, in the United States, we are trying to recapture what we have destroyed—fast, efficient, comfortable mass rail transportation and convenient supermarket access to juicy, ripe, edible tomatoes.

Perhaps the best example—other than print on paper—of the disdain for old technology in the mindless rush to the new is radio. Daniel Boorstin eloquently illustrated this recurring phenomenon in the preservation documentary, *Slow Fires*, by asking who, in the dawn of television, would have predicted that we would walk around in the future with radios in our ears! Even more unforeseen is the amazing resurgence of a popular new application—radio mail—to enable laptop computer users to read their e-mail and surf the Internet without the need for telephone wires.

Another example is the widely-hyped current buzz-word, the Digital Library, and, like all buzz-words, is hopelessly imprecise. To the computer scientists at the National Science Foundation, who created a multi-million dollar program to encourage research into the digital library concept, the term signifies the technological infrastructure. To librarians, who hoped to apply for these grants, the term implies the storage and management of digital information. To university administrators, seeking to restrain library costs, it means cheap and easy ways to provide access to knowledge resources traditionally held in libraries. And, to the humanist scholar, it means the demise of the book.

I do not believe the issue of the future is a simple one of book vs. digital signal, as both humanists and technological gurus contend. I believe that print-on-paper technology through its primary manifestation—the book—has served and will continue to serve a complex, multi-faceted role in human society. But we must also acknowledge that the book has serious limitations which can be eliminated by digital technology so that its strengths will continue to serve many useful purposes for a very long time to come.

What must change to enable the humanities and the culture of the book to flourish in the 21st century are our human systems for organizing, managing and financing continuing access to knowledge. We cannot graft digital technology onto our existing system of social organization—the very fabric of our society—which has been designed around the characteristics of print-on-paper technology. We must recognize the painful but inevitable fact that digital technology will topple our traditional organizational boundaries, make economic formulas and management systems obsolete and, in general, as the cliché has it, change the paradigm. If we are going to use technology in an intellectually responsible manner, rather than be overrun by the profit imperatives of commerce or dazzled by the transient charms of ever-changing technology, it is essential that the community of humanists shape their future by looking carefully at the strengths and weaknesses of the printed page and digital technologies in order to combine the best of both. It is an interesting irony to me that our information systems of the future are being conceived and built by engineers who, as university librarians know, rarely use libraries. But even more devastating is the fact that, until recently, humanists, the heaviest users of the documented human record, have passively permitted them to do it.

In an editorial, "Wired Science or Whither the Printed Page?" published in *Science*, the authors, an IBM researcher and a chemist, make the point that the scientific community needs to ask some very hard questions about electronic publishing and conclude that "the issues are too important to the scientific community to be left only to those who are developing the technology."[1] I believe it is equally imperative for the community of humanists to shape their future by looking carefully at the strengths and weaknesses of the printed page and digital technologies in the effort to combine the best of both.

It has become a truism that one constant of our contemporary society is change; however, we sometimes fail to recognize the distinction between "change" and "transforming change." A truly revolutionary and transforming change wrought by digital technology is its capacity to create, disseminate, store and use information in multiple formats and media, thus releasing us from the constraints of the printed page for teaching, learning and scholarship.

In his book, *The Twilight of Sovereignty: How the Information Revolution is Transforming our World*, Walter Wriston describes the challenge of the information age.[2] In the industrial age, the technology defined the task. We built huge and sprawling steel mills which then dictated the way steel was made. We built large libraries to house books and journals, which dictated the way scholarly research and instruction were conducted, and we built a huge infrastructure of educational institutions which defined the way we taught and learned. However, in the Information Age, the intelligence of the hardware and the software, combined with sophisticated communications systems, now permit the task to define the technology.

We have grown so accustomed to the fact that scholarly information requirements and habits have been essentially shaped by the constraints of centralized systems of libraries and computer centers that we no longer acknowledge or even comprehend that this is so. The course of instruction and the pursuit of research have been largely dependent upon the availability of information resources and services determined by the central allocation of institutional funds and decisions regarding the use of those funds by librarians and computer specialists. The increasing decentralization of technology and access to information available to the student and the scholar at the workstation in a variety of media and formats means that we can now respond in kind to customized inquiries and searches. We can provide the book when that particular format will expand the mind; we can provide machine-readable text when that format will contribute to different ways of thinking about a problem; and we can provide the tools with which to convert numbers and texts into graphic images to enhance the learning process.

Since print-on-paper technology has defined the tasks of both information providers and users for centuries, there is a lot we need to learn about how we use—and want to use— knowledge unconstrained by the limitations of print-on-paper and then design our systems accordingly. Providing customized services will be our foremost challenge in the 21st century. Before we rush headlong into the digital age, we need to deepen our understanding of how we learn, how we create works of the intellect and the imagination, and how we will provide continuing widespread access to that intellectual and cultural heritage to sustain and promote the principles of a free society.

A first step is to look beyond both the deification of the book and the inflated and all-encompassing rhetoric surrounding the glories of the Internet and the World Wide Web. Now that we have the capacity to create, disseminate, store and use information in many different formats, we must assess the strengths and weaknesses of both book and electronic publications. In the past the book has performed, perforce, all these functions, and, as we have learned in the acid paper debacle, some better than others.

As a representational artifact of human creativity, the book is both a carrier of textual knowledge as well as an object of art when used to combine text, image, bindings and elegantly produced paper. At the same time, the rapid replication capability effectively destroys our traditional copyright balance between stimulating creativity and providing broad access.

The digital representation can combine text, image, sound and video to embody non-linear creations of the human imagination, new forms of knowledge, and enhanced properties of visualization enabling new styles of learning. The book is flexible and portable, but it is also a cumbersome dissemination medium in a fast-lane electronic society. Its physical properties often require scholars to travel to it, rather than the other way around. The lengthy publication process inhibits rapid dissemination of new knowledge.

In contrast, digital technology has an infinite capacity for global transmission, but requires a sophisticated, coordinated and costly communications and computing infrastructure. Electronic publications are site-independent and portable to the laptop (which is not yet quite the same as a book); they promote sharing and collaborative ownership, eliminating costly duplication.

The book, as we discovered with the adoption of the new technology of acid paper in the mid-nineteenth century, is a frail archival medium. As collections grow, books require massive spaces on prime real estate locations convenient to users, although remote storage locations are becoming necessary from both economic and space availability realities. Large collections are difficult to browse, particularly when split between remote storage and easily accessible sites. Our analog minds probably still consider the book the best format for use for many activities because it is flexible, portable, inexpensive and easily annotated. On the other hand, electronic media are much better for activities such as referencing databases, hypertext searching, and providing linkages to related materials. The digital signal also easily combines multimedia and can be inexpensively translated into a customized medium—paper, magnetic tape, CD-ROM, etc. And, although acid paper has a shelf life of only 30-50 years, the shelf life of electronic media is even shorter—and far worse, the short shelf life of the medium is greater than the life cycle of the hardware and software required to gain access to the knowledge stored therein.

It seems abundantly clear from this brief analysis that there are compelling reasons for humanists and librarians to work together to complement the limitations of paper with the strengths of digital technology so that we gain more than we destroy. Technology has always been a two-edged sword. In the mid-nineteenth century, the spread of literacy outran the supply of rags to make durable paper. In the enthusiasm for the power of the cheap new acid-paper technology to make knowledge widely accessible, we failed to comprehend that the acid paper carried within it the seeds of its own destruction. One hundred years later, with huge portions of our library collections crumbling into yellow snow on their shelves, we finally recognized our folly.

In 1989, the National Endowment for the Humanities, in an extraordinary act of national and international leadership, stepped up to this challenge. Today the National Endowment for the Humanities' preservation program stands out as an example of a national agency dealing with a cultural issue of importance to all citizens. It is currently enabling research and demonstration projects to explore the advantages of digital technology for rescuing deteriorating brittle books. This new technology permits unprecedented physical and intellectual access, economical off-line storage of the original content with the option of individual enhancement to counteract faded inks, foxing, cockling and other blemishes, and best of all, conversion back into acid-free paper copies.

Because digital technology releases us from the constraints of print-on-paper, offers us more choices than in many cases we want, and essentially undermines the viability of our traditional systems for creating, disseminating, storing, using and paying for access to knowledge, we stand once more on the threshold of a major cultural and technological revolution. Our traditional organizational structures, autonomous institutions reflecting the characteristics of print-on-paper technology, are no longer adequate for successful management of digital technologies. To coordinate on a broad national scale the thoughtful consideration of the many critical issues affecting humanistic studies in an electronic world, new and unprecedented collaborative relationships will be needed, requiring extraordinary leadership from organizations such as the National Endowment for the Humanities.

Each new technology has fueled an enormous proliferation of knowledge and created at the same time an even greater challenge to transmit that knowledge to those who follow us. Brittle books are causing us enormous expense to preserve a portion of our crumbling intellectual heritage but at least we have had fifty to one hundred years to mobilize our efforts. Electronic media is not that forgiving. In a recent study by the Commission on Preservation and Access and the Research Libraries Group, the task force concluded that the best use of its work will ultimately be to "heighten awareness of the seriousness of the digital preservation problem, its scope and complexity -- and its manageability. There are numerous challenges before us, but also enormous opportunities to contribute to the development of a national infrastructure that positively supports the long-term preservation of digital information."[3]

Thus the greatest threat of digital information technology is its terrifyingly transient nature. In all the furor among humanists about the destruction of the culture of the book and the reluctance to acknowledge the limitations of print-on-paper, we have badly misplaced the emphasis. The book, as one medium in a multimedia environment, will be with us for a very long time. The critical challenge of the future lies elsewhere. In a technologically driven society which seeks to expand access to knowledge, to enhance individual learning styles and push ever forward the frontiers of human knowledge, the central concern for the humanist must be to influence actively, persuasively and eloquently the design of information systems. These systems must reflect our philosophical and educational values, and must match medium and format to the intellectual inquiry. Above all the information systems of the future must insure broad and continuing access to the human record. Otherwise, the fleeting and feckless demands of the mass market will govern the fate of the humanities in our society. Without knowledge of the past and the present, our future will be dim indeed.

Notes

1. Winograd, Shmuel and Richard N. Zare. "'Wired' Science or Whither the Printed Page?" *Science,* 269(August 1995):615.

2. Wriston, Walter B. *The Twilight of Sovereignty: How the Information Revolution is Transforming Our World.* New York: Scribner, 1992.

3. *Task Force on Archiving of Digital Information, Preserving Digital Information.* Washington, D.C.: The Commission on Preservation and Access, Unpublished Draft Report 1995, iii.

Continuum, Not Revolution

by Sir Charles Chadwyck-Healey

A large oval room lined with books in the Imperial Public Library, St. Petersburg in 1812. In the center of the room a splendid pink sofa. On it lies Ivan Andreevich Krylov, librarian of the Rossica department. Sometimes dozing, exhausted perhaps from telling extravagant tales about himself, or from his work on the collection and editing of Russian folklore. But when awake, immensely knowledgeable and helpful to his patrons. To find a book there was no need to consult a catalog; ask Krylov, who knew the location and contents of 30,000 books in his library. Generous and expansive, reclining on the pink sofa, he would point to the book with the words, 'Go there, dear sir, and take what you want'.[1]

To library patrons in this century such a scene would be a fantasy. The guard-book catalog in hundreds of huge volumes or the card catalog in phalanxes of cabinets became the bastions that kept the readers at bay - from the books and from the staff. In Britain and Europe closed stacks exacerbated the reader's feeling of powerlessness, reaching its peak in the Round Reading Room of the British Museum Library in the early 1970s. Here, and still, the guardbook catalog encircles the enquiry desk - like a rampart. Behind it staff used to huddle, fearful of the hordes of visiting scholars who descended every summer. Beset by staff shortages and the essential inaccessibility of the stacks, the books were issued slowly and reluctantly, if at all. The reader had plenty of time for his fantasies in those days.

Ian Willison describes the catalog as one of:

> the four techniques of control of the natural anarchy of the book world that have since become fundamental for research library administration: catholic acquisition (in the case of non-Greek texts largely by translation); rationalization of the format, and even the content, of books; systematic author and subject cataloging, linked with more finely edited bibliography (the *Pinakes* of Callimachus); and a continuing conservation program, largely in the form of recopying.[2]

Only the qualifications in parentheses indicate that Willison is not only talking about research libraries in the 1970s but also the post-Lyceum Alexandrian Library four centuries before Christ. It is extraordinary that the immense developments in technology, from printing to electronics, have left these four basic precepts unchanged. Even conservation by recopying is the method embraced in the late twentieth century through major conservation microfilming programs. In the Library of Alexandria, scribes hand copied manuscripts; at the end of two millennia after Christ, keyers in the Philippines and India hand key the texts of printed books for much the same reasons - for preservation of the text and for better distribution - which is now electronic.

It was a nineteenth century development in information technology - the steam press that led both to the later crisis of acidic wood pulp paper, which has required the wholesale copying of texts for preservation and to the ever growing size of collections in nineteenth and twentieth century libraries. Much of the development of technology and systems in libraries has been in response to this. Krylov's patrons were fortunate that the collection, which was named after M. E. Saltykov-Schedrin by Lenin's wife in 1932, was within the comprehension of one gifted man, an excellent bibliographer who did much to develop the Russian collection in what is still the State Public Library. But Krylov himself would have understood the need to develop a cataloging system such as that created by Anthony Panizzi for the British Museum Library between 1834 and 1850 for what had become one of the largest and fastest growing collections in the world.[3]

This is not an attempt to examine the intellectual content of library catalogs, the first efforts at subject cataloging, the influence of Panizzi's British Museum Rules which crossed the Atlantic to be used by Charles Coffin Jewett in the library of the Smithsonian Institution but which failed to penetrate Oxford, nor the relative merits of Dewey and Library of Congress Cataloging Rules and the extent to which they advanced or held back the eternal quest for better access to the contents of books. This is to look at the catalog as a physical entity, first in book form, unnecessarily large and heavy volumes because of the empty space that had to be left for later additions, and the need for thick strong pages on which the slips could be pasted. And then in card form, a system that could be kept under reasonable control if one 5 inch by 3 inch card could represent one book or, better still, one journal run. Unfortunately, the card catalog began to grow exponentially when each book had to be represented by multiple cards for author, title, subject and shelf list. But the card catalog had its own redundancies as profound as those of the guardbook. Space had to be left in drawers - if only to let in fingers. The more drawers, the more solid the wooden or metal structure had to be, and there needed to be plenty of space between the cabinets to allow users to stand at fully opened drawers while others passed by.

And then in the 1970s the miracle of compression began - with the lowly microfiche reader; lowly because it really was low-tech; a handful of moving parts, no electronics, a screen, a mirror, a lens and a light. Yet the microfiche whose images it projected was the creation of a remarkable marriage of optics and electronics, the COM recorder, which converted ASCII characters to images projected on to film at a rate of 4.5 pages per second. The quality of the image was so superior to that of the conventional microfiche camera that it could be reduced 48 times rather than the normal 24 times, a 400% increase in the amount of information that could be stored on each 6 inch by 4 inch sheet of film, and an important further step in the reduction of the size of the catalog. This low-tech terminal was most people's first introduction to computerised information in the library yet was as static as the book or card catalog, and had the same redundancy with the need for duplicate copies offering alternative points of access via title and subject. It was only a matter of time before the cost of networking and the cost of terminals fell to a point where a library could afford to connect the library user directly to the catalog. The catalog hall became a thing of the past because the entire catalog of the largest library could be situated anywhere that there was a connection to the network.

And so technology has liberated the reader so that he can enjoy the same freedom as that enjoyed by Krylov and his patrons. The Librarian of Harvard College can sit on a sofa in his spacious office and, with a laptop on his knee connected to the networks, locate any book or journal in the library. Can he or she offer it to the reader with the same generosity as Krylov? It is in the USA that the great research libraries have opened their doors the widest, allowing in readers from the local community and from neighboring educational institutions. But now that libraries offer access to their catalogs via the Internet to anyone in the world who is connected, it is inevitable that the information flow out of the library will not stop there. It is striking the extent to which the electronic information revolution has been seen by librarians and library users as heralding a new era in which information will be free. Why this should be so is not clear and may be an example of hope over reason even amongst the most reasonable people. Yet it may be a deep-seated instinct that the time has come to overhaul the commercial restrictions imposed on the dissemination of information which are there to protect the publisher and in certain instances the author, which generally made sense in a world of print on paper but which seem to get in the way of achieving the ideal embodied in Krylov's, 'Go there, dear sir, and take what you want'.

'Now Barabbas was a publisher', said the poet and prolific writer and critic Thomas Campbell, and there is not much love for these carpetbaggers engaged in a branch of commerce which has only been separately identified over the last two hundred years. Librarians aware of the symbiotic relationship between themselves and the publishers scrupulously observe the sometimes labored and even impractical contractual restrictions currently imposed upon them. They are content to bide their time because they can see that the publishers themselves are beginning to move towards different kinds of contractual relationships in order to provide access to their publications in ways that have never been seen before.

The miniaturization of the catalog went a small way towards alleviating another late twentieth-century crisis in libraries: that of lack of space. The cataloging hall often in the most important part of the library could be liberated for something else. In the 1960s the solution to the space problem was to build bigger libraries; in the 1990s lack of money is matched by a lack of will to build, with a sense that there has to be a better solution. The new British Library, the largest and most expensive public building to be built in London in the twentieth century, is not quite large enough even before it opens. This failure to come to terms with the physical reality of such a library is as much cultural as financial. The cost overruns are horrendous but have come about because of the reluctance of successive governments to accept the consequences of the decision to house an entire national collection in central London, resulting in two inflation-ridden decades of hesitation and delay.

The long-term solution is now seen to lie in the conversion of information into electronic form. It cannot be the whole solution because books and journals will continue to be produced on paper for years to come. The Mellon Foundation is funding the JSTOR project to convert the back-runs of journals in the social sciences found in college libraries into scanned image form. The purpose of this project is primarily to enable medium sized libraries to find more space within existing buildings. At the same time, hundreds of journals are now being published in electronic form accessible over the Internet. Most of them have paper clones taking space on the shelves, but for how long?

Two entirely different solutions in less than thirty years: The problem itself is seen as one that belongs exclusively to the second half of the twentieth century; the post-war information explosion coupled with the world-wide increase in literacy and in higher education. We think of the constraints and problems that we are faced with as being particular to our time and are then surprised to find that they are problems that have had to be faced before. The 'electronic revolution' gives us new tools to solve problems which were solved by other methods in the past.

In Balzac's *Illusions Perdues,* published in 1837, the solution to the space problem is not to build bigger buildings but to make smaller books.

His hero David Séchard:

> If we could but succeed in making cheap paper of as good a quality, the weight and thickness of printed books would be reduced by more than one-half. A set of Voltaire, printed on our woven paper and bound, weighs about two hundred and fifty pounds; it would only weigh fifty if we used Chinese paper. That surely would be a triumph, for the housing of many books has come to be a difficulty; everything has grown smaller of late; this is not an age of giants; men have shrunk, everything about them shrinks, and house-room into the bargain. Great mansions and great suites of rooms will be abolished sooner or later in Paris, for no one will afford to live in the great houses built by our forefathers. What a disgrace for our age if none of its books should last![4]

The passage on the changing technology of paper-making with its heart-felt cry of the late twentieth century, 'What a disgrace for our age if none of its books should last!', is followed by: 'Dutch paper - that is paper made from flax - will be quite unobtainable in ten years' time.' And thus Balzac, who had substantial though unprofitable experience as a licensed printer, appears to foresee the consequences of the changes in paper-making that arose from the most important development in information technology since the beginning of printing - the steam press.

The steam press had the same symbolic importance for its age as the 'information highway' has for ours. Philip James Bailey in his poem published in 1858 *The Age; A Colloquial Satire*, a lengthy diatribe against the Press writes:

> Be sure, ye doleful dupes who daily dream
> That God will save the world by rags and steam;[5]

The steam press had a visceral presence that is not shared by the Internet. Anyone who has seen a very large web offset printing machine cannot fail to be moved by its sheer size and sense of power. Couple this with the steam engine, the noise, the billows of steam, the smell of machine oil, hot metal, and ink, and it is not surprising that it was seen in the nineteenth century as a monster, devouring not only paper but even men. Pressmen lost fingers and arms, and sometimes even lives. William A. Bullock of Philadelphia, who in 1865 invented the first machine to print from a continuous web of paper, was killed by being caught in the driving belt of one of his own presses.

The Times installed the first ever steam press in 1814. Emerson, visiting *The Times* in London in 1848, wrote:

> 'Meantime, it attacks its rivals by perfecting its printing machinery, and will drive them out of circulation: for the only limit to the circulation of the "Times" is the impossibility of printing copies fast enough; since a daily paper can only be seasonable for a few hours'.[6]

The importance of the steam press lay not only in its ability to produce large numbers of copies but also in its ability to produce large numbers of copies in a short space of time. This is also a characteristic of electronic information dissemination. It is not just that information can be disseminated to many people but that it can be disseminated so quickly. In the nineteenth century, it had been the newspaper publishers who benefited most directly from the *speed* of the press; in the age of the Internet it is less clear that newspaper publishers will benefit, unless they boldly embrace the new technologies as a few have already done. Book publishing dynasties also flourished in the nineteenth century fed not only by the new printing technology but also by the growth of a national and international communications network - the railroad and later the electric telegraph. In Britain Routledge's 'Railway Library'[7] was an example of the relationship between the demand for entertainment and the communications network, but it was in France in the 1830s that there emerged a publisher with an instinctive grasp of the opportunities that were made possible by the changes in technology, communications and in society itself. This insight was matched by a ruthless single-mindedness and a use of mass market techniques that make most book publishers of the last fifty years seem positively old fashioned.

The publisher was the Abbé Migne and we are indebted to R. Howard Bloch for his revelation of the true nature of Migne's Ateliers catholiques in Paris.[8] Migne to most people seems an unlikely candidate for such a claim. The very nature of the books he published, religious texts and the writings of the holy fathers, hardly seem to us to be the stuff of mass market publishing. Migne is associated in most scholars' and librarians' minds with the *Patrologia Latina* in 221 volumes and the *Patrologia Graeca* in 166 volumes. Together they form the single most important collection of the works of medieval authors and while there are now new editions of many authors, for the majority, the *Patrologiae Cursus Completus* remains the standard reference source over a century after its publication.

Migne's output in forty years was extraordinary. The two Patrologiae total one million pages yet represent only half his output. He personalised his achievement with the boast that he never took a days holiday and worked 16 hours a day, but it was his understanding of the new mass production techniques and his exploitation of his workforce that enabled him to be so productive. He concealed the 'modern' nature of his publishing activities by conceiving them along the lines of the cathedral, the monastery and the scriptorium, but then went on to say:

'Then too the hand of a monk of yesteryear could not copy in three years what is done in the Imprimerie catholique in a single minute'[9]

and in one of his advertisements wrote:

Steam is harnessed to mechanical power, and their force of production is such that they can give birth to 2,000 volumes in quarto every 24 hours.[10]

Yet he sought to legitimise his publications by using the image of monks laboring in the Ateliers catholiques. He drove his workers hard and showed little charity to them or to the outside world. Even the Paris police considered him to be an oppressive employer and the fact that there is so much information about him in the archives is due to the complaints laid against him by his workers. He deliberately recruited workers from the most dispossessed sectors of the population including, according to the Goncourt brothers, 'defrocked rogues' and 'death cheaters'.

All this productivity would have merely resulted in large numbers of unsold books if his sales and marketing organisation had not been equally inspired. He was a master of the publisher's 'puff' and all those publishers who have assembled prestigious academic boards, whose sole purpose is to add respectability to reprint or microform sets and who persuade distinguished scholars to describe their publications in glowing terms have much to learn from the Abbé Migne. Migne first sent out a questionnaire to 5,000 members of the clergy to determine which editions he should include in the Patrologiae in order to create the impression that this was a work derived from the advice he had received from the very people who would be his prime market. Thereafter came the 50,000 congratulatory letters which he claimed to have received though some of them, according to Bloch, seem curiously similar in style to Migne's own publicity blurbs. He approaches the Press and openly offers payments or books in return for editorial comments that praise his publications, to a point where paid-for advertisement and independent editorial merge into one.

This approach is matched by an equally aggressive pricing policy that embraces every device that latter day publishers use to induce libraries and the general public to part with their money sooner rather than later. Even the long statement in Latin on the title page of every volume of the *Patrologia Latina* contains two references to the inexpensive nature of the volumes and what good value they represent (*oeconomica* and *pretii exiguitas*). He prepares the foundation of his pricing structure by pointing out that the volumes in the two Patrologiae if bought separately would cost over 100,000 Francs. If the purchaser bought both he would pay only 2,500 Francs, five Francs a volume or six if he bought each series separately. Then there were other perks such as pre-paid postage on the letter placing the order, extended credit and delivery to the door for each volume - important for a priest living in a remote rural area.

At the beginning of 1838 the price goes up to 6 Francs a volume while the first 1,000 subscribers pay 1,000 Francs a set; thereafter 1,200 Francs a set. A purchaser who pays in advance for Migne's entire *Bibliothèque universelle* in 2,000 volumes pays 8,300 Francs rather than the list price of 10,000 Francs.

A priest who only wants to buy one of the Patrologiae is encouraged to find a colleague who will buy the other or, better still, both will order a pair each and then sell on the unwanted sets to others, while any priest who takes it upon himself to sell a subscription will receive a free volume or a free set for every ten sets sold.

What is interesting is not the detail but the concept. Migne used modern production processes and questionable commercial practices, such as not paying royalties, to enable him to sell his publications at very low prices and then uses direct mail merchandising techniques to sell very large sets of these individually inexpensive volumes. He adopted these techniques at the very time that the communications network made it possible to reach the entire population of France quite easily and quickly - the first telegraph line was established the year the first volume of the Patrologiae was published. He focused on a clearly identified market -- priests and seminarians and their related institutions -- and used modern communications methods to reach them. Migne understood how he could use such technological advances to increase his sales and incongruously within the text of the *Patrologia Latina* itself, in the Preface to volume 218, is the statement:

> Quantum inde tempori parcetur! Cedit via ferrea et aeria; vim illam aemulamur cui electrum nomen dedit![11]

which Bloch translates as, 'What an economy of time! It's better than the railroad, even the balloon, it's electricity![9]

Migne saw the *Cursus Completus*, particularly the Indices as a shortcut to the study of the Christian past comparing his publications to the tunnel blasted through Mount Cenis, 'greater even than the construction of ten cathedrals'.[13] How warmly he would have welcomed the electronic edition of the *Patrologia Latina* which makes that path even smoother and easier, and have found some equally grandiose example with which to compare it!

Today publishers are offered the same opportunities as Migne, brought about by radical changes in information technology. Production methods are being revolutionised; the very medium of publication changed while methods of delivery to mass markets are transformed by the Internet and the potential of cable transmission into every home. Yet as in Migne's time when most publishers remained firmly in the eighteenth century, the majority of publishers today still seem to regard the 'electronic revolution' as much a threat to the comfortable old ways of the past as an opportunity that beckons to the future.

That this conservatism is a fundamental part of human nature seems to be demonstrated by the reaction of the scriptoria to the establishment of printing almost 600 years ago. While some must have recognised the impact of the new technology of printing and have prepared to shut up shop or become printers themselves, others just carried on handcopying their books while in England some scriptoria even used Caxton's printed works as sources because they were easier to copy from.

The first printers had embraced a revolutionary new technology and yet in many ways were themselves entirely conservative in putting it into use. They copied existing manuscripts rather than commissioning new works and used the format of the manuscript book as their model for the printed book. The first printed books had no title pages, foliation was rare and quires were marked with signature letters. There was no technology for printing capitals or illuminations so when a book was printed it was handed over to a rubricator to be finished off. Nor should conservatism in itself be condemned. Nicholas Jenson, the great French printer working in Venice in the late fifteenth century, created one of the most beautiful early typefaces by directly copying a humanist script. Contrast this with the works of Migne, whose pages are crammed with a graceless and near illegible typography.

The publisher of electronic texts knows that he is at a turning point yet looks to the past for guidance on how to approach the future. The electronic edition of the Patrologia displays the text as if the screen was the page of a book using a typeface which is more traditional and certainly more elegant than the stunted face used by Migne. The electronic edition has a greater sense of spaciousness in its leading and its margins because it does not have the constraints of space that Migne was faced with because he had to cram the words on the page to keep down his production costs.

Everyone in electronic publishing today has grown up under the influence of printed text - even though radio, television and film are also important influences, and it is probably impossible to conceive the presentation of an electronic publication in a way that does not to a great extent imitate the conventions of the printed page. The browsers on the Internet use classic serifed typefaces and most users prefer the scanned image that exactly imitates the printed page to monotonous and difficult to read blocks of ASCII characters. Reading a long text on the screen is tiring and printing it out onto paper to read elsewhere awkwardly straddles the technologies in the same way that early print was combined with hand drawn rubrics. Digital technology will one day enable the creation of an entirely new publication that will combine text, sound and both still and moving images in three dimensions and will not require a separate screen for viewing/reading. We can imagine that this may be achieved by a device like a pair of lightweight spectacles on the lenses of which text and images are displayed with built in earpieces for sound, and a microphone for interactive commands. The data will be stored separately and transmitted so there will be no wires or heavy storage devices.

Like the publisher the librarian has to address the uncertainties of the new technology as did earlier generations at each previous technological turning point. The 'natural anarchy' that Willison refers to is with us on the Internet. The bibliographic control of digital information which can so easily be corrupted presents great intellectual challenges for the librarian. Maintaining collections comprised of publications each of which incorporates text, moving and still images, and sound will require an expert understanding of the technical aspects of the library stock, while digital data on whatever storage medium present long-term conservation problems which have hardly been addressed. Far from being marginalised by the existence of wide area networks delivering information directly to 'patrons', the role of the librarian remains as central to the control and distribution of electronic information as it was for the manuscript book over 2,000 years ago. Without the mediation of the librarian 'patrons' or 'end-users' will be overwhelmed by a chaos of information whose real value and even whose identity they will find difficult to determine. These technological advances will also have an important influence on the commercial relationships between publishers, authors, librarians and end-users. Already there are library consortia buying joint access to electronic databases, something that never happened with other media. The importance of these changes may in the end be as great as the changes in the technology itself. The Internet is already 'opening' libraries to the world, and we can hope that librarians of the future will once again address their patrons wherever they may be with the generosity of spirit embodied in Krylov's, 'Go *there*, dear sir, and take what you want!'.

Notes

1.   I was told this story on a visit to the library in February 1991. I am grateful to Natalia Volkova for confirming that it is recorded in the history of the library. See also: Stuart, M. *Aristocrat Librarian in Service to the Tsar: Alexsei Nicolaevich Olenin and the Imperial Public Library* New York, 1986.

2.   Willison, Ian R. *On the History of Libraries and Scholarship.* A paper presented before the Library History Round Table of the American Library Association, June 26 1979. Washington: Library of Congress, 1980. p. 9.

3.   Chaplin, Arthur Hugh. *GK: 150 years of the General Catalogue of Printed Books in the British Museum.* Aldershot: Scolar Press, 1987.

4.   Balzac, Honoré de. *Lost Illusions.* translated by Ellen Marriage. New York: Avil Publishing Company, 1901. p. 114.

5.   Bailey, Philip James. *The Age; A Colloquial Satire.* London: Chapman and Hall, 1858. p. 92; as it appears in *The English Poetry Full-Text Database,* CD-ROM. Cambridge: Chadwyck-Healey 1994.

6.   Emerson, Ralph Waldo. *Essays and Lectures.* Cambridge: Cambridge University Press, 1983. pp. 909-910.

7.   The first shilling volumes in the 'Railway Library' were published in 1848 at the same time that W. H. Smith & Son were acquiring bookstall rights on railroad networks. Mumby, F. A. *The House of Routledge 1834-1934.* London: George Routledge, 1934; and *Archives of George Routledge & Company 1853-1902,* microfilm. Bishops Stortford: Chadwyck-Healey, 1974.

8.   Bloch, R. Howard. *God's Plagiarist.* Chicago: The University of Chicago Press, 1994.

9.   Bloch, p. 15.

10.   Bloch, p. 15.

11.   Migne, Jacques-Paul, ed. *Patrologia Latina,* vol. 218, col. IV; as it appears in *Patrologia Latina Database,* CD-ROM. Alexandria: Chadwyck-Healey, 1995.

12.   Bloch, p. 126.

13.   Bloch, p. 4.

Achieving Preferred Library Futures in Turbulent Environments

by Richard M. Dougherty

Readers of this festschrift, I'm sure, already understand that academic librarianship, as we know it, faces an uncertain future. But uncertainty need not translate into a gloom and doom scenario. In fact, I am personally optimistic about future prospects for libraries and librarianship as long as librarians step forward and provide leadership as change-oriented managers. Richard De Gennaro, the person we honor in this festschrift, epitomizes what I mean by a leader who has been successful in creating organizational environments that are hospitable to change.

It is my belief that successfully managing change will be the principal challenge library leaders and managers will face in the decade ahead. The most successful leaders will be those best able to create and implement new and exciting service visions for their organizations. To assist those who seek to create new futures for their organizations, I am presenting a powerful visioning/planning process. It is a process that is being used by complex organizations in both the public and private sectors.

Overview

The process is known as "preferred futuring." It derives from the work of Ronald O. Lippitt, a noted social scientist, and his colleagues.[1] This is a process which helps organizations create exciting futures, and can be used as the basis for a formal strategic planning process.

Have you ever been part of a group that came together to plan, but before anyone realized what was happening, you began to debate the problems and frustrations of the present? As a result the group could not find a way to leave the present and leap into the future and imagine futures that truly excited the group. The preferred futuring process described in this paper makes such leaps a normal expectation.

Preferred futuring is a multi-step process that begins with a look backward at past accomplishments and then reviews present activities in order to identify what is working and what is not. Groups quickly move from the past and present to an initial glimpse of the internal and external factors that are likely to impact and shape the organization's environment over the next few years. Following this "environmental scan" the group engages in exercises designed to expand its expectations and to prepare for the visioning process that follows. All of these steps are intended to make it easier for a group to project images of the futures it prefers, and to convert those images into a working vision. Once the futures are described, attention turns to the more practical aspects of creating action-oriented strategies. The final step is to ensure that milestones of progress are celebrated on a regular basis.

A Change Model

Preferred futuring assumes that organizations are ready to undertake a change process to achieve new goals. Although this paper focuses on visioning and action planning, readers should keep in mind that understanding what is necessary for change to occur in an organization is of fundamental importance. Visions will not be achieved if change can not be managed.

The literature is rich with change models. One model that I have found to be particularly useful is based on the work of Beckhard and Harris.[2] Their model suggests that three conditions must be present for change to occur. One, people must be dissatisfied with the current situation. Two, the organization needs to create a vision that is shared. Three, a change strategy that incorporate milestones of progress is necessary. Beckhard and Harris also suggest that if any one of these conditions is absent, organizational change efforts will be especially difficult.

The Need to Act

Many librarians currently acknowledge the need for change, but a surprising number of libraries have not yet initiated comprehensive programs of change. The most common explanation for inaction is "we do not have the resources to initiate new programs." This is a classic case of acting penny-wise and pound foolish. Inaction on librarians' part will only increase the chances that libraries will become obsolete as service organizations.

Many librarians, however, have embraced the philosophy of Total Quality Management (TQM). While TQM serves as an effective strategic for achieving change, it is not a process that normally leads to a transformational change that allows an organization to reinvent itself. But realistically speaking very few academic libraries are trying to "reinvent" themselves because users, particularly faculty, continue to embrace past library traditions. In short, many faculty have not been enthusiastically supportive of dramatic changes in libraries. While these attitudes may be changing, library leaders must be sensitive to the views of stakeholders such as faculty.

Fortunately, incremental changes under certain circumstances can lead to a transformational change. For example, the first generation of OPACs, while a dramatic change from their predecessors, were still only a digitized version of their paper-based predecessors. However, as improvements such as linked databases and expanded serial holdings information were added incrementally, the enriched OPAC gradually transformed our concept of bibliographical control and access.

Another explanation for inaction is that the majority of faculty and staff simply do not feel the need to endure the "pain" of change. For example, until recently academic teaching hospitals rarely engaged in programs of change; they only began to recognize the need for change when the fear of managed health care overwhelmed existing organizational inertia and resistance.

Another obstacle to change at academic institutions is the inability of leaders to articulate exciting visions that generate a broad base of campus support and motivate the campus to act. The need to act, however, is recognized by some leaders in higher education. Gerhard Casper, the president of Stanford, told a group of educators at a recent meeting that "higher education leaders [must] prepare themselves for high-tech competitors of the future by defining their institutions' value to society." He predicted that "...distance-learning technologies would have 'a profound impact' on universities as they blur the lines between high school, college, and advanced degrees and enhance the shift to 'life-long learning.'[3] The need for librarians to act is no less critical--with or without the comfort of "adequate" resources.

The easy answer--not having adequate funding--is obvious and often too simplistic. There has never been enough money to do all that we would like to do. The no-money explanation is often only an excuse to avoid action. This timidity, in my judgment, is a failure of leadership.

Acknowledging the Past

The first step in a preferred futuring process is to identify and recognize the accomplishments of the past. In my view there is much to celebrate. It would be easy to compile an extensive list of accomplishments, for example: automated and outsourced cataloging, new reference service models, automatic acquisition plans, fax augmented ILL, WWW Homepages, etc.

Most librarians viewed such changes as positive developments, but it is important to remember that there are also staff who mourn the passing of activities they have devoted their professional lives to performing. If you think I exaggerate, talk with a cataloger who watched the passing of original cataloging or the reference librarian who is no longer able to interact with information seekers who approach the desk.

At the time such changes were occurring, the mourning staff were probably viewed as change resistors who needed to be set aside. It is instructive to understand why staff may resist changes. For example, using support staff at a reference desk may make sense economically, and for some reference staff this new service model is embraced with enthusiasm. They view the change as an opportunity to take on new and more challenging tasks. But for others the removal of professionals at the reference desk violates a value they hold dear. For these professionals one of the reasons they chose reference as a career track was the opportunity to interact with patrons.

We have found that staff whose contributions are adequately and publicly acknowledged find it easier to break from the past and accept new challenges. Therefore, it is important that change agents not forget to celebrate the contributions of staff whose jobs are about to change or even disappear. Managers must also avoid giving the impression that these staff, whose functions are being phased out or reorganized, wasted their professional careers. The objective is to acknowledge past contributors and provide a vehicle that eases the transition to new jobs and challenges.

Assessing the Present Situation

Before trying to create exciting new futures, it is important for groups to assess the present. We want to learn how people feel about the organization. What is working? What is not? This review helps to establish a realistic baseline upon which one can build a new future. It is also an opportunity for staff who are participating in a change process to blow off steam and come to realize they are not the only ones who have concerns about what is going on or what is not going on. A recent experience should illustrate what I mean.

A group of librarians, faculty, administrators and technologists were engaged in a brainstorming session. Many seemed extremely proud of the quality planning that had been accomplished in recent years. The academic administrators were particularly enthusiastic. Paradoxically, the same brainstorm also produced a number of comments suggesting that others were frustrated with planning. These were mostly faculty, computing professionals, and librarians who cited the chronic failure to actually implement plans; they wanted action! The outcome of this brainstorm provided a more realistic view about how people *really* felt about the present situation.

When assessing the present, a group must guard against becoming distracted by the problems of today. I have frequently observed groups who become mired in discussions of the day-to-day problems. When this occurs, groups find it extremely difficult to leap into the future. Usually the blocks to creative thinking revolve around a lack of resources and/or conflicting priorities, i.e., too much to do and not enough time to do all that is needed. A properly structured preferred futuring process helps groups avoid this common trap.

Trends, Events, and Developments

A look at emerging trends, events, and developments can be accomplished by conducting a form of an "environmental scan." This exercise can generate a rich array of data, particularly if a critical mass of staff participate in the process. We often forget that staff, regardless of their position in the organization, have ideas and opinions of value to offer.

An environmental scan can be used in a variety of ways. For example, a scan can be used as a reality check as planning for the future progresses. One group I worked with recently identified budgetary constraints as one of the chief economic factors that would shape their future. While the group was not overjoyed with this prospect, they agreed that this was a likely development. Later, during the action planning step of the process, it became obvious that several of the group's proposed actions were contingent on obtaining new money. When the group was reminded of what they had said earlier in the scanning exercise, they stopped and rethought their funding assumptions. Instead of discarding their ideas, they became more innovative in their search for resources, e.g., reallocation of existing resources, grants, fund raising, etc. As a result the action plans were more realistic than they might have been otherwise.

An environmental scan can also facilitate two-way communication within an organization and help a group to arrive at a common understanding of how staff view the near-term future. For example, a scan involving the entire staff might be the first time a janitor or a junior secretary has interacted with senior staff and administrators and learned what they believe to be the important emerging trends, events and developments. Conversely, this exercise might also be the first opportunity for the administrators to hear what junior staff believe the future has in store.

An environmental scan can be structured in a variety of ways. Some scans focus on the library itself, but since the fortunes of academic libraries are usually closely linked to those of their parent institutions, a library scan should also reflect campus-wide trends, events, and developments.

During the last recession, some librarians believed that when the national economy came out of its doldrums, campus budgets would became healthier, and consequently the library would also benefit. However, as the economy rebounded, most campuses and their libraries did not seem to benefit. In a recent scan, a group of librarians identified several factors that suggested that constrained campus budgets would remain the norm. The factors they identified include:

- higher education has become so expensive that it is now beyond the means of many families who traditionally expect to send their children to college;

- more and more colleges are acknowledging a "tuition ceiling"; some are even finding ways to reduce the cost of an education;

- government funding of research and student support programs has leveled out or is declining;

- higher education is not presently a high societal priority (which is indeed ironic since college graduates continue to have financial advantages in the job market over those who do not attend college);

- technology is reshaping the nation's educational infrastructure and hastening the introduction of distance education programs.

It is possible that the outlook predicted by this group will prove inaccurate, but the exercise was valuable because it helped them to create a common set of planning assumptions. This process is one step in what Peter Senge calls building a "learning community."[4]

Stretching our Horizons

People conditioned by problems and frustrations currently confronting them often have difficulty projecting their thinking into the future. Fortunately there are strategies that can be employed to help them expand their horizons. One technique for broadening thinking patterns is to listen to a successful innovator talk about his/her successes. Success and innovation can be contagious. Such presentations can be inspirational; the ideas shared can also serve as the foundation upon which new innovations can be visualized.

Creativity exercises are another way to broaden the thinking of a group. In a recent workshop, a reference librarian from a small college talked about a centralized reference service that effectively integrated staff expertise and technology at a single service point. Since several of the other participants were struggling with similar organizational issues, the ideas shared by this librarian served as an eye opener for the others. As the group talked about such innovations, I realized they were ready for a leap into the future.

Images of the Future

Lippitt's preferred futuring process is quite different from processes that are intended to predict the future. Lippitt's intent is to stimulate creativity--a right brain activity; whereas, futurists such as Eric Toffler specialize in predicting the future--a left-brain activity. I am not arguing for one approach or the other; I only want to point out that "preferring futuring" and "predicting the future" are different processes. It was Lippitt who pointed out that the products of a preferred futuring process could be used as a prelude to a more rationale strategic planning process.

Preferred futuring utilizes a variety of brainstorming techniques. The objective is to identify the futures that are preferred. When people engage in this process they sometimes find it difficult separating what they *predict* will happen from what they *prefer*. For example, they predict that virtual libraries will replace "brick and mortar" libraries within ten years. But what they prefer is a library environment that supports full utilization of technology but retains the library as a place. Their preferred vision is the campus library serving as the campus hub for information services. Our task is not to judge between the two visions but to help groups to create the visions that excite them.

One consortium I worked with created the following working vision from their brainstorming: "We are a dynamic organization dedicated to serving and enabling our new community and to providing the best access to available information resources." Now that they have a vision of a future that excites them, the key question becomes "how will they achieve our preferred future?" The next task will be to identify the strategies and tactics that will enable them to convert their images of the future into realistic action plans.

Connecting Images to Action

Tools that will help convert images of the future into concrete action of today are available. One easy and effective tool is the forcefield analysis developed by Kurt Lewin.[5] A forcefield analysis helps to identify the forces that are most likely to both drive and inhibit efforts to change. Again, brainstorming techniques are used to identify existing (or perceived) forces. The information generated with forcefield analyses is used as the basis of action planning. Action planning exercises can be structured so that the actions become progressively more and more specific.

These processes can be used to create very specific plans. In fact the objective of action planning is to reach a level of specificity that allows one to ask and answer: who, what, when, where, how and why questions. For example, who will do what, when will we next meet, what procedures will we use, what resources will be needed, etc.? This level of action planning can also serve as the foundation for a re-engineering project.

"Re-engineering" or "reinventing" organizations are two popular concepts. To some people the terms mean streamlining organizational structures by eliminating layers of management, to others the terms refer to rethinking how tasks are performed and who performs them.

Action Strategies

TQM and the concept of continuous improvement of processes and procedures has gained many advocates among librarians. A library can use the tools of TQM to develop and implement action plans that help a library progress closer to its preferred futures. Among the principles postulated by Edward Deming, a TQM pioneer, is the belief that the customer is always right, and that management problems should always be looked at through the eyes of customers.[6] Moreover, staff are rarely the source for production problems, but rather the procedures workers are expected to use are flawed.[7]

In a TQM work environment, the aim is to improve the efficiency of the work performed. In fact, TQM is often referred to as a "continuous improvement process." The tools associated with TQM are simple to use and have been available to libraries for many years, e.g., flow decision chart, flow process chart, floor layout charts, Pareto charts, fish-bone charts, etc.

The principles of TQM can also be combined with the commonsense approach of work simplification. The principles and tools of work simplification can be used to review the efficiency, effectiveness, and rational of most library policies and procedures.

To illustrate, consider how interlibrary loan and borrowing (ILL/ILB) procedures lend themselves to review and analysis with the tools and techniques of continuous improvement and work simplification. Most ILL/ILB units still maintain a combination of paper and digital files. Moreover, ILL/ILB is a labor intensive set of activities. A couple of years ago an ARL study pegged the average ILL/ILB transaction cost at an ARL library to be slightly more than $29.00-- not a trivial cost.[8]

Some libraries responded immediately by employing the tools of continuous improvement to streamline operations and eliminate redundancies, e.g., eliminate paper files. One library I visited recently eliminated virtually all of its paper files. The only remaining paper record is a numerically arranged archival file that must be maintained for legal reasons.

This library began its re-engineering project by reviewing its ILL/ILB from the point of view of its customers. They asked: "what do we know about the behaviors of users who seek documents?" They came to the conclusion that they knew quite a bit.

- users tend to consult the most accessible sources of information (e.g., personal collections and the collections of close colleagues; everyone today seems pressed for time);

- users will turn to the easiest sources to use (most people do not know how to use libraries effectively);

- users will turn to the systems that they believe will produce the information when they need it (I want what I want when I want it).

- when money is an issue, users will seek the most affordable price available.

Although there is nothing startling about these observations, this focus on user tendencies helped staff to reassess its policies and procedures to reflect user preferences.

Celebrating Progress

One critical element of a preferred futuring process is the need to recognize and celebrate progress. While giving recognition might seem obvious, it is a step that is too often overlooked or downplayed. The need to recognize progress generously and often is particularly important in our culture because we seem to have very short attention spans. If we can not point to progress quickly, workers tend to become discouraged and do not stay the course.

The current interest with the concept of virtual libraries illustrates what can happen when we fail to build milestones of progress into our planning processes. While a virtual library environment will eventually become a reality, most experts agree it will take years before virtual libraries are able to provide services comparable with today's libraries. While the vision of a virtual information environment is exciting, what do our organizations do in the meantime? How do they prepare for the virtual environment? What are the milestones of progress? How will staff know that they are on the right track during these transition years? William Bridges, a well-known change management expert reminds us that managing the transitions in an evolving environment presents one of the most demanding challenges organizational leaders currently face.[9]

Conclusion

Preferred futuring is a powerful process. It is also a versatile problem-solving tool. It can be used for a variety of purposes, some broad and expansive, others focused and specific. I've used it to help groups create new organizational visions, new public service visions, restructure library units, design collaborative projects, and discover new roles for staff.

But most importantly the preferred futuring process can enhance a leader's ability to initiate and manage change. I believe that the leaders of the emerging generation will be those who are best able to lead their organizations through periods of turbulent change.

What about the future of librarianship? It is easy to get caught up in the hype of technology and the wonders of the WWW. The world of the Internet is indeed exciting. Nonetheless, I still believe that if librarians continue to hold dear traditional values such as equity of information, intellectual freedom and patron privacy, and if we do not forget that librarianship is a service profession, and that our standing in society is based on our ability and willingness to assist all who seek help, regardless of their financial means, we will succeed as a profession and as professionals.

Notes

1. Lippitt, Ronald O. "Future Before You Plan." *The NTL Managers' Handbook.* Edited by R. A. Ritvo and A. G. Sargent. eds. Arlington: NTL Institute, 1983. pp. 374-81.

2. Beckhard, Richard and Reuben T. Harris. *Organizational Transitions: Managing Complex Change,* 2nd ed. Addison-Wesley Publishing, 1986.

3. "Stanford's Casper: Colleges Face Competition in High-Tech Era," *Chronicle of Higher Education,* April 28, 1995. p. A50.

4. Senge, Peter et al. *The Fifth Discipline Fieldbook: Strategies and Tools for Building a Learning Organization.* New York: Doubleday, 1993.

5. Lewin, Kurt. "Quasi-stationary Social Equalibria and the Problem of Permanent Change." in *The Planning of Change.* Edited by W. G. Bennis, K.D. Benne and R. Chin. eds. New York: Holt, Rinehart, Winston, 1969. pp. 235-238.

6. Deming, Edwards. *Out of the Crisis.* Cambridge: MIT Center for Advanced Engineering Study, 1982. pp 167-182.

7. Deming, pp 77-85.

8. Mackey, Terry and Kitty Mackey. "Think Quality! The Deming Approach Does Work in Libraries." *Library Journal,* May 15, 1992. pp. 57-61.

9. Bridges, William. "Managing Organizational Transitions." *Organization Dynamics.* New York: American Management Association. p. 24-33.

Research Libraries and Foundations

by Warren J. Haas

University research libraries have been transformed over the past four decades. Operating methods have been fundamentally changed; new and complex relationships have been established among libraries and with all components of the communication structure, creating irreversible dependencies; and the range of resources and services offered has greatly expanded. Also, the number of these libraries, measured by Association of Research Library membership, has tripled to more than one hundred and their annual combined operating cost has risen from $25 million in 1955 to $1.7 billion forty years later.

The transformation from a long era of stability to the dynamic and often uncertain present was initially stimulated by the rapid increase in college and university enrollment following WW II; by the related expansion of academic research, which in turn generated demand for comprehensive research collections in both established and new subject fields; and by the conviction that the embryonic information technology should be exploited to improve all aspects of library performance. The unusual -- one might say unprecedented -- challenge for libraries forty years ago was to expand space and resources quickly enough to meet user expectations. Over the succeeding years, the pressure to improve library performance has maintained its momentum, driven by a succession of events -- financial constraints that predictably followed a decade or so of affluence, growing sophistication of library management, and the insatiable expectations of users in what has become the digital age.

In general, research libraries and their parent universities have responded well to needs and opportunities, but not all of the initiative was from within. Important assistance came from beyond the universities as well -- federal and state governments provided funds for program expansion (PL480 and support for area studies collections, for example), for organizational innovation (such as New York State's Regional Reference and Research Library program and comparable ventures elsewhere), and for physical facilities. Most notable, both for its inventiveness and its consistency, was the leadership of a few private foundations -- especially those that saw the opportunities for higher education and research libraries inherent in the times and were also willing to provide the risk capital required to test ideas and encourage action. This essay is written as a reminder of the importance of the contributions of these foundations to the development of academic research libraries over the past forty years.

While our focus is on only a dozen or so private foundations, those that were a clear force in shaping the research library of today, it is important to acknowledge the role of others as well. There are more than 30,000 private foundations in the United States. The great majority, by virtue of individual program definitions, are restricted in their grant making activity to one or a few specified areas of interest or to a narrowly defined geographical area or region. Of the 30,000 foundations, only about 500 granted significant funds to libraries and information service organizations during 1994, the most recent year for which information is available. While the 1,700 grants made to libraries totaled nearly $200 million (about 2 per cent of all grants), 60 per cent of that total came from only 25 foundations. Many of the largest grants were for physical facilities, capital campaigns, and computer equipment and related costs. These funds granted to individual libraries were obviously of great importance to the recipients, and often were the difference between stagnation and a new life, but by and large they reflect rather than precipitate the kinds of change libraries have undergone.

In order to describe the work of foundations as change agents within the limits set for this essay, a few of the key turning points for libraries have been selected as examples. Drawing on the fortune of participation and memory (for much of the detail of the place of foundations in this history has not been well recorded), it is hoped that the factual record will be enriched. Following the "history", an observation or two about what the future might hold for the library-foundation relationship will be offered.

The first, and in many ways, the most far-reaching foundation action of the type here explored was the creation of the Council on Library Resources (CLR) by the Ford Foundation in 1956. While the history of CLR is not yet written, its agenda has, from the beginning, been the future of all libraries. For more than 20 years, Ford was the sole source of support for CLR, providing $29 million in unrestricted funds in periodic payments of $5 million to $8 million. The stated purpose of CLR was "to aid in the solution of library problems' and this is still the underlying objective, even though Ford's general funding formally ended some years ago. Ford did not prescribe or approve CLR program directions, leaving that responsibility to a self-perpetuating governing board initially constituted by the foundation. Ford did receive annual financial and substantive reports, and on at least one occasion established an external review committee to assess the programs and progress prior to a making a large renewal grant. In addition, a senior Ford program officer was designated to provide assistance and guidance when requested.

This is not the place to review the details of CLR activity over nearly forty years -- they are in the widely distributed annual reports and the many publications of the Council and are fully described in the reports of its hundreds of institutional and organizational grantees. There are several aspects of the Council's operation, however, that should be identified because they have served both library and foundation interests well. First, there has been a remarkable consistency in the CLR program over the years. Bibliography, especially simplification, standardization and cooperation in the production and sharing of bibliographic records has, in one project after another, been a CLR hallmark. The protection and preservation of collections has had equal billing, starting with funding of early projects in the field of paper chemistry to explore the causes of the deterioration of book paper and subsequently to press for the production and use of acid-free paper in the manufacture of books. The application of technology to library operations and services was a primary interest of those who made the initial case for establishing CLR to the Ford Foundation, and the cause has been pursued for four decades, from the development of an automatic page turner for possible use in televising text to experiments with hypertext for expediting user searches of textual and image databases. While libraries have been the focus of CLR activity, the driving force from the beginning has been the principle of equitable access to information.

The profession of librarianship demanded attention as well, given the growing complexity of the processes involved. Studies designed to forecast the future were commissioned, library schools were urged to explore their role in preparing students for a new and demanding set of professional specifications, and librarians were encouraged to undertake research projects pertinent to their work or to continue their formal education through graduate programs in appropriate subject fields. Finally, among the continuing CLR programs was the improvement of library management, an effort that, over the years, took many forms and involved many organizations and institutions, resulting in the managerial sophistication of many in the profession today who, individually and collectively, are able to function effectively in a constantly changing environment.

In addition to persistence in addressing library operating problems, CLR has helped to promote discussion and understanding of issues and options among user communities, university administrations, and librarians. This was accomplished by structuring a representative CLR Board and by establishing a system of program advisory groups composed of specialists from within the profession, representatives of many academic disciplines, senior university officers, and when appropriate, private foundation representatives. This effort, in turn, prompted academic organizations such as the American Council of Learned Societies and the Association of American University Presses to include librarians in certain of their deliberations.

The Ford Foundation, in establishing CLR, opened the way to a new level of national collaboration in the work of recasting, not only the libraries of forty years ago, but the information structure that underlies all of scholarship, research and learning. Much of the effort underway today transcends CLR itself, but the seeds were there, often to be picked up by other foundations that used the Council and other organizations as agents for change.

On July 1, 1977 the Ford Foundation brought to an end its twenty year role as sole supporter of CLR. The Carnegie Corporation of New York and The Andrew W. Mellon Foundation both made unrestricted grants to CLR to supplement the balance of Ford funds. At the same time, Carnegie and Mellon, with the support and participation of Ford, established what came to be called the Foundation Library Committee. Richard Sullivan, Vice President for Finance and Treasurer of Carnegie, served for five years as the moving force behind the development of the Committee and John Sawyer, President of Mellon, often set the pace for foundation involvement in library ventures. The Committee expanded from four or five foundation representatives to more than a dozen during the ten or so years of its active life. Representatives from the Library of Congress and the National Endowment for the Humanities were included as well. The members met quarterly for several years, usually in the offices of one of the foundations. The purpose of the meetings was to provide information about library developments and concerns to the representatives of the participating foundations. No proposals for funding were presented, but on occasion the interest of one or several members in a projected activity was obvious. On a number of occasions, guests from one or another organization were invited to meetings to discuss subjects of interest to the group. The existence of the Committee and the opportunity to be reliably informed about library matters did much to stimulate interest in libraries among foundations, and there is strong evidence that, as a result, foundation funding for libraries increased, both through CLR and directly to individual libraries and library service

28

organizations. It is no accident that the decade of the Foundation Library Committee marked the high point of foundation participation in the evolution of the country's research library structure.

Two or three brief case studies, starting with preservation, will serve to illustrate the importance of the link between foundations and libraries. While the matter of book paper deterioration received some attention in the 1930's, it was not until after W.W.II ended that the subject began to receive serious attention. The work of W.J. Barrow at the Virginia State Library came to the attention of CLR soon after the Council was established, and a series of paper chemistry projects were funded that established beyond doubt that paper manufacturing processes were at the root of the problem. CLR also funded a series of studies sponsored by the Association of Research Libraries to begin to quantify the magnitude of the problem and to set forth a national plan for the preservation of research library materials. By and large, findings and plans had little immediate effect, probably because, as the magnitude of the problem became clear, the cost and complexity of a solution was overwhelming for an already overtaxed library community.

Looking back, the turning point for preservation, from years of fact finding and planning to what is now more than a decade of action, came when John Sawyer decided that the time was ripe to "try again". A meeting was convened by Mellon in New York in May, 1979, bringing together about twenty individuals involved in paper manufacturing, publishing and library preservation activities to gather information about book paper and to begin the process of identifying ways to address the prospective aspects of preservation. In effect, the result of the meeting was to separate the past from the future as a first step in setting a course of action. From that point on, work on the preservation problem moved into high gear. The Committee on Production Guidelines for Book Longevity, chaired by Herbert Bailey, Jr. of the Princeton University Press, was formed and during the next two years gathered information about the use of acid-free paper and binding materials. The report of the Committee, "Book Longevity", which appeared in *Publisher's Weekly*, drew national and international attention and gradually stimulated constructive action by paper and book manufacturers. The report also served as a base for the development of a national standard for permanent paper for printed library materials.

The profile of preservation on the national agenda grew quickly. In collaboration with the Association of American Universities and the American Council of Learned Societies, CLR sponsored a series of Forums on library related issues, one of which was preservation. Prompt action was urged by the participants, and a sub-group assisted CLR staff in preparing a work plan. Subsequent discussion with the Foundation Library Committee early in 1984 prompted a suggestion from Arnold Shore of the Exxon Education Foundation that a regional preservation facility be created, that a national planning effort be undertaken, and that a public information program be established. A $1.5 million grant to CLR from Exxon was used to establish the Mid-Atlantic Preservation Service; to fund the work of the Committee on Preservation and Access which resulted in the report "Brittle Books", which, in turn, became the source document for the Commission on Preservation and Access; and finally, to cover a portion of the planning cost for the film *Slow Fires*. The film, which was funded by Mellon and the National Endowment for the Humanities, did more in its hour-long running time on public television than did all the diligent work of previous years to bring the problem of preservation to the public eye, nationally and internationally. Ultimately, *Slow Fires* was an instrumental element in encouraging government action, including Congressional hearings and the creation and funding of the Office of Preservation within NEH.

Foundation contributions, financial as well as intellectual, to the cause of preservation have continued in support of the work of the Commission on Preservation and Access, but that portion of the history can be picked up at another time. The brief and far from complete record outlined above will suffice to underscore the contribution of foundations to what is one of the important library success stories of recent years.

The "journal problem" is the match of preservation in complexity and intractability, and provides another example of the importance of foundation-library collaboration. The Mid-West Library Center was established immediately after W.W.II by the "Big Ten" Universities and the University of Chicago to collect and store "important but little used materials" held by the member institutions. Subsequently expanded in membership and renamed the Center for Research Libraries, the Center began (with grant support from the Carnegie Corporation) to collect as they were published many of the less used but still important journal titles in a few scientific fields on behalf of its members. Perhaps because demand for articles was modest and subject coverage narrow, a critical mass of activity was never reached and concern by publishers was restrained. Several state journal access systems also developed (Minnesota, for example), but, by and large, these simply provided statewide access to the collections of state universities by public and academic libraries and probably had little effect on subscriptions. By the early 1970's, however, the "journal problem" was obvious and well defined. Financially pressed research libraries were faced with maintaining thousands of subscriptions to journals whose numbers and costs rose at unprecedented rates. Librarians were caught in the middle, between faculty that required immediate access to the literature of their specialty, regardless of cost, and the constraints of budgets and space. Responding to widespread concern, the National Commission on Libraries and Information Science (NCLIS), in 1977, recommended that the Library of Congress assume responsibility for developing and operating a U.S. national periodical center. The Library of Congress turned to CLR to manage the planning function (with the cautious provision that the plan not focus exclusively on the Library of Congress). Funds for the project, totaling $115,000 were provided by eight foundations in the first collaborative undertaking by members of the Foundation Library Committee. A technical development plan was incorporated in the report *A National Periodicals Center*. The report and subsequent discussion failed to solve the problem. Initially, prospects improved with the House inclusion, in 1979, of a new Part D in Title II of the Higher Education Act to establish a National Periodicals Center as a non-profit corporation. But legislative efforts finally failed as a number of publishers expressed strong opposition, and some segments of the library community (either concerned about an additional Federal presence in the information structure or feeling that technology would soon solve the problem) gave only cautious support. Strong reservations surfaced within NCLIS itself, especially among the publishing and commercial information service members of the Commission.

Fifteen years later, the problem has not gone away. The library literature of the past decade has reported resentment about a system that has universities "buying back", in the form of costly journals, the product of their own, institutionally funded, research. Given the capabilities of present computer and communications technology, the validity of the idea of printed journals has been questioned, since it is the articles within that are the substantive entity. As the problem persists, so has the interest of the foundation world. The Andrew W. Mellon Foundation, with the direct involvement of its President, William G. Bowen, has recently established a non-profit agency, JSTOR (journal storage), to test performance, utility, and costs of an electronic database of selected scholarly journals. Perhaps the time is finally right for a collaboration of foundations, libraries, scholars and publishers to solve the journal problem.

These examples of foundation supported library programs with national impact are only indicators. Every major undertaking funded by CLR over the years -- improving library management; developing a comprehensive, computer based, national bibliographic service; enabling participation of national library leaders in the development of cooperative projects with the Library of Congress; and expanding bibliographic access internationally, along with many other ventures -- was, in effect, funded by foundations. Additionally, tens of millions of foundation dollars have been granted, for similar purposes, directly to organizations such as the Research Libraries Group and the Association of Research Libraries, to regional affiliations of academic libraries, to independent research libraries, and to the scholarly partners of libraries, the university presses. For four decades, private foundations enabled research libraries to transform themselves from essentially self-contained entities to the core element of what, one day, might become an integrated system of scholarly communication. The system is imperfect and still evolving; many segments of society are, as yet, essentially unaffected, but the promise of participation is real.

Intense competition and conflicting objectives are evident in the politics of shaping the structure that enables the information age, but there seems to be no technical constraint on what can be done. It is not clear whether the end result will be shaped largely by force, accident, or national intent. Whatever the process, from the point of view of libraries and their allies, there are principles of equity and performance to be upheld, economic realities to be recognized and dealt with, and, most of all, a long established and unquestioned sense of purpose to be pursued. A difficult and promising time lies ahead, and much help will be required.

The number of private foundations committed to supporting the structure of scholarly communication and, especially, the continuing transformation of research libraries has declined in recent years. In fact, only a few of the members of the Foundation Library Committee still retain a significant interest in library matters. Examples are The Andrew W. Mellon Foundation, which continues to give personal and financial support for work in several key areas, and the W.K. Kellogg Foundation, which is now funding projects intended to improve the professional education of librarians and the services of large urban libraries.

The lower level of support for academic research and scholarly communication generally reflects the fact that, over time, foundation program changes are the rule rather than the exception. New leadership inevitably brings new interests, a review of past performance and a rearrangement of funding priorities. Rising expectations for education, the importance of research as the base for economic well being, and the realities of global integration were forces that clearly shaped the programs of the largest foundations for twenty or more years after the end of W.W.II. These matters all had an obvious information component. Other, less comprehensive issues were added over time -- population control, the agricultural innovation required to feed the world population, degradation of the environment, etc. In the most recent decade, social problems of many kinds and the proliferation of advocacy groups for a wide range of narrowly defined causes have greatly influenced foundation programs. In a sense, foundations have been pressed to pick up where government has failed and, as a result, much of established value has fallen by the wayside.

There is no good reason that the information base on which civilization rests should be of transitory interest to foundations or anyone else. Libraries are the keystone of the information structure, whether in the print or digital age: they link individuals to what is known. Because of their centrality, libraries and their supporters have an obligation, on a continuing basis, to pose the questions that need attention and to persist in their search for support. At heart, the issue is not the well being of libraries, but the well being of individuals. Libraries of every kind are society's invention to ensure, for each of those individuals, the opportunity for equitable access to needed information.

How might libraries go about restoring foundation interest in the work they seek to do? The best advocates are those directly concerned, for they have both the information required to make the case and the power of their conviction. For the most able of these, providing for the future is as important as serving the present.

An important beginning might be to report carefully and critically on what has been accomplished thus far. Every foundation expects and usually receives reports on work accomplished with grant funds. Most are read and all are filed, usually an adequate conclusion for clearly defined projects. But the funding identified in this essay -- risk capital for experiment and innovation -- is of a different kind. It is not so much the completion of a project that is the measure, but rather the actual effect of the work done over time. A way should be found for libraries (perhaps with help from their users) to assess the impact that foundation funding has had on library operations and service and on the quality of our evolving information structure. In essence, foundations should know in some detail and with some certainty what their financial and staff investment over the past four decades has helped to accomplish. Further, it would be useful to give the assessment appropriate visibility. This is a difficult assignment, but it can be done. A series of case studies would allow for analysis and presentation suited to the nature of the topic and might well identify matters for further attention. In short, foundations are one of the few sources of risk capital for innovation in education-related activities. Evidence justifying their investment might well help make the case for continuing participation.

If foundation interest in libraries is to be restored and expanded, and, equally important, if libraries are to flourish and meet their obligations in the context of the new information age, each kind of library -- research, collegiate, urban public library, rural community library, etc., -- needs to prepare its own blueprint for the future. These agendas must be set in a time frame, they must be precise and purposeful, the means and conditions for success must be clear and realistic. A commitment to appropriate collaborative action must be made, since no sector of the information structure can succeed in isolation. Full participation by libraries and their strongest allies, their users, in the work of shaping the future is the surest protector of library objectives and principles in an aggressive and competitive arena.

Once again, as it was some decades back, this may be time to make the case -- expansively, precisely, and visibly -- for attending to the future of libraries. Private foundations can respond.

Bibliography

A National Periodicals Center. Washington: Council on Library Resources, Inc., 1978.

Annual Report. Washington: Council on Library Resources, Inc., 1957 - present.

Birkerts, Sven. *The Gutenberg Elegies.* New York: Fawcett Columbine, 1995.

Bowen, William G. "JSTOR and the Economics of Scholarly Communication." Washington: Council on Library Resources Conference, 1995.

Brittle Books. Report of the Committee on Preservation and Access. Washington: Council on Library Resources, 1986.

Grants for Libraries and Information Services. New York: The Foundation Center, 1995. *Foundation Giving: Yearbook of Facts and Figures on Private, Corporate and Community Foundations.* New York: The Foundation Center, 1992.

Samuels, David. "Philanthropic Correctness." *The New Republic,* September 18 & 25, 1995.

The Evolving Research Library: A Memetic View[1]

by John Kupersmith

There is a quiet revolution going on in academic research libraries. It is a revolution that is being driven by powerful economic and technological forces. It started in the 1960s and is now accelerating at an extraordinary rate. By the end of this decade, libraries will be profoundly different from the libraries we have known and used in the past. To be sure, the buildings, bookstacks, and the reading rooms will still be there, but the library will be fulfilling its mission in new ways, and it will be making extensive use of new information technologies.[2]

One thread that runs through the work of Richard De Gennaro, in both his writings and his day-to-day actions as a manager, is the application of a finely tuned common sense to the sometimes abstruse world of libraries. In a time of profound change for research libraries, he has helped not only to set our agenda, but also to shape our shared idea of what a library can and should be, and what a librarian can and should do.

The "nascent science" of memetics[3] is a useful tool for understanding and interpreting both the overall paradigm shift in research libraries and De Gennaro's contributions to it. This theory holds that ideas, in effect, have a life of their own and can be viewed as "information viruses." In 1976, Richard Dawkins proposed that ideas behave in much the same way as genes, surviving through replication as they move from one mind to another (or many others). Although there had been previous speculation on this subject, as early as William James in 1880,[4] Dawkins formalized the analogy in modern terms and coined the word "meme" to describe the concept:

> I think that a new kind of replicator has recently emerged on this very planet. It is staring us in the face. ... Examples of memes are tunes, ideas, catch-phrases, clothes fashions, ways of making pots or of building arches. Just as genes propagate themselves in the gene pool ... so memes propagate themselves in the meme pool by leaping from brain to brain via a process which, in the broad sense, can be called imitation. If a scientist hears, or reads about, a good idea, he passes it on to his colleagues and students. He mentions it in his articles and his lectures. If the idea catches on, it can be said to propagate itself, spreading from brain to brain.[5]

A meme can be as simple as the first four notes of Beethoven's Fifth Symphony, as wordlessly powerful as the photographic image of Earth from space,[6] or as complicated a "meme-complex" as the doctrine of Jeffersonian democracy. These instances demonstrate that memes can profoundly affect the lives of people whom they "infect." When expressed in human behavior, the consequences of harboring and transmitting a particular meme can be essentially healthful (e.g., respect for the elderly), or unhealthful (e.g., ethnic cleansing).[7]

Memes live in human minds, which taken collectively form an environment variously called the "infosphere" or "ideosphere" (both analogous to biosphere).[8] Within this environment, memes are transmitted through all the channels of human communication: word-of-mouth, exemplary behavior, formal education and training, art, music, published literature, libraries, the mass media (including, for good or ill, sound-bites), and electronic communication networks. Those individuals who are especially skilled at meme transmission, and/or have especially potent memes to transmit, may be called trend setters, opinion leaders, or change agents. A meme can spread very slowly (e.g., the metric system in the United States) or very quickly (e.g., Beatlemania). It can influence an individual or a great number of individuals, such as the citizens of a country or the members of a profession.

Dawkins also pointed out that memes compete with one another very much as genes do, and specifically that they compete for our attention. His argument has a natural appeal to those who live and work in meme-rich environments and suffer from information overload:

> The computers in which memes live are human brains. Time is possibly a more important limiting factor than storage space, and it is the subject of heavy competition. The human brain, and the body which it controls, cannot do more than one or a few things at once. If a meme is to dominate the attention of a human brain, it must do so at the expense of "rival" memes. Other commodities for which memes compete are radio and television time, billboard space, newspaper column-inches, and library shelf-space.[9]

Later commentators have expanded on the idea of meme competition; its application to religion, politics, and social movements; and the factors which contribute to an idea's survival. According to this theory, a meme tends to survive and proliferate if it contributes to the fitness of the individual and the group, if it proves to be reliable in interpreting events and making predictions, if it is easily learned and transmitted, and if it encourages its "carriers" to behave in ways that reinforce its existence and integrity.[10] Institutionalized forms of meme competition include advertising, scholarly communication, and the democratic election process. Memes can compete for credibility in explaining a phenomenon (e.g., evolution vs. creationism) or for influence in shaping peoples' actions (e.g., altruism vs. selfishness). One term for an especially significant meme victory, affecting the way people think and behave, is "paradigm shift."

A concept as broadly applicable as that of memetics can obviously be used for a variety of purposes. Taken to extremes, it can lead to a view of humanity in which people are seen as mere hosts and vectors for information viruses. Daniel Dennett illustrates this reductionist approach with the wry slogan, "A scholar is just a library's way of making another library."[11] Applied with judgment and moderation, however, the "meme about memes" provides a useful perspective on the history and development of ideas.

The Research Library Meme

> The stereotype of libraries as static, unchanging institutions is no longer valid if it ever was. Libraries, and especially large libraries of record, are necessarily and by nature conservative institutions. However, in the last hundred years they have

demonstrated a remarkable ability to grow, to adapt to changing conditions, to meet new demands, and to implement new technologies.[12]

The meme (or more correctly, meme-complex) which defines our concept of the research library has undergone a number of fundamental changes during the past four decades, changes which have become widely institutionalized. These trends are generally recognized and have given rise to a voluminous literature, some of which has recently been documented in a valuable review by Karen Drabenstott.[13] As her compendium shows, numerous memes have been vigorously competing to replace the traditional, print-based, collection-intensive, non-networked storehouse model of the research library. Major variations on the general theme include the digital or electronic library, the virtual library, the library without walls, and the hybrid library combining printed and computerized information. There are also variations in how the new paradigm would be funded and phased in, how it would interact with the larger world of electronic publishing and scholarly communication, and how it would relate to users and their needs.

These emerging memes have been successful in claiming the attention of many librarians, academics, and others to the extent that they provide a framework for understanding advances in information technology and a strategy for applying these new capabilities in a feasible, cost-effective way. Those library models which could most easily be symbiotically linked to "co-memes" such as the wired campus and the scholar's workstation have had particular strength, especially when the time came for them to replicate among university administrators and scholars. Those models which could be clearly communicated, and demonstrated in pilot form, have been able to replicate more successfully than those which could not be so easily transmitted. When implemented even partially, the meme of the computerized library tends to be highly self-reinforcing since it involves special equipment, training, activities, rewards, and in some cases, new job titles and descriptions.

Looking at the way this meme competition has affected actual institutional practice as libraries have modified their identities and operations, some general patterns emerge. The following discussion focuses on transitions in the perceived business of libraries, the ways in which libraries do business, and the role of library staff and their relationship to users.

The Business of Libraries

> In the future, the size of a library's collection of conventional materials will matter far less than it does now. The question is no longer how many volumes a library has, but how effectively the library can deliver needed resources from a wide variety of sources to users via the new technology. The emphasis is shifting from collections to access. ... Technology is making the resources within the library available beyond its walls, and the resources beyond its walls available within the library.[14]

While the majority of library acquisitions and usage still involves local collections of printed books and journals, as we enter the late 1990s most libraries have made at least partial transitions from storehouse to gateway, or more correctly, added the latter role to the former.

Networked bibliographic utilities, interlibrary loan systems, and document-delivery services provide increased access to what is not held locally. A growing variety of CD-ROM and on-line products, though far from perfect, provide both indexing and full text to a remarkably broad range of library sizes and populations. In some cases, libraries are designing their own products and their own gateways. The access paradigm has changed to the point that significant amounts of library research--though not necessarily all of it--can be conducted without an actual visit to the building. The dominant meme that appears to be emerging, at least in this stage of history, is that of the hybrid or "bionic"[15] library, serving users' needs with a combination of formats, resources, and technologies.

How Libraries Do Business

> Providing access to information will be the principal goal and activity, and coping with technology and change will be the principal driving forces of the emerging information age library.[16]

> We are entering a new era and the only way libraries can conserve what they have built in the past and perform their vital mission in the future is by innovating. ... The greatest challenge facing library leaders in the next decade is not to implement new technology, it is to implement new entrepreneurially oriented management structures and cultures in our ailing industrial-age libraries.[17]

Technology, and the memes associated with it, have affected libraries' internal processes as much as their external manifestations. Technical services departments have seen dramatic changes from an emphasis on bibliographic control based on local cataloging, to an emphasis on expedited access based on shared cataloging, minimal-level cataloging, and other devices. Public services are undergoing equally basic transformations, as discussed in the next section.

Throughout the library, the advent of e-mail and networked file-sharing has changed the way staff do their work, speeding up communications and flattening hierarchies in the organization through the subtle but powerful meme of electronic democracy. Alternative forms such as matrix structures and cross-functional project teams have been tested and in many cases found to contribute to organizational fitness. The growth of worldwide e-mail, listservs, and newsgroups has broadened librarians' long-distance professional communication from something that happens occasionally on the telephone, or periodically at conferences, to something that happens as part of one's daily work, through constant immersion in a global community.

As it has annihilated many of the constraints of distance, technology has also compressed our sense of time, affecting how librarians approach tasks and how they plan for the future. The accelerating pace of change in our environment, and the rapid development and prototyping capabilities of systems such as desktop publishing and the World Wide Web, have fostered a shift from long timeframes to short timeframes. The meme of a flexible, hands-on, action-oriented workstyle (as spread, for example, by the infectious Tom Peters)[18] has helped to shape this behavior. This is not to imply that technological change and speeded-up work are easy; anxiety, confusion, and stress are very much part of the process.[19]

Some of the library profession's own organizations and institutions have functioned as influential memetic agents, fostering changes in prevailing techniques and styles of library administration. For example, the Academic Library Management Internships and other programs of the Council on Library Resources have provided a number of librarians with new ideas and experiences.[20] The ARL Office of Management Services, through its training programs and publications, has exposed thousands of librarians to memes often transplanted from the mainstream business and management literature.[21]

Staff and Users

> We need to reexamine our ideas about what the real needs of our users are and what it takes to satisfy them. ... Just as American business is going back to basics, rediscovering the importance of the factory floor and production, so we librarians need to go back to basics and rediscover that our main function is serving users .[22]

Few memes have been embraced as passionately by librarians as those of the client-centered library and the importance of understanding, serving, and in some cases educating library users. Few aspects of library operations have been analyzed, agonized over, and redefined as thoroughly or as often as reference service. This is one of the most intense areas of meme competition in the profession, with alternative models--traditional, consultative, proactive, deskless, and machine-assisted, to name a few--vying for attention and adoption.[23] The perfect formula eludes us (if indeed there could ever be such a thing), and experimentation flourishes as the validity of these rival memes is tested.

What should not be overlooked in all this ferment is that the relationship of staff and users is changing in very basic ways. A growing minority of users are picking up a new meme, moving from the role of supplicant to that of participant in the library process. Searching computerized catalogs and databases, performing full-text and -image retrieval, and dialing in from their own offices and homes, they bring a richer background to their dialogues with librarians. Meanwhile, staff are (sometimes reluctantly) giving up their identity as isolated experts on bibliographic arcana and assuming the role of co-learners, approaching the reference and teaching situations as a joint exploration with their colleagues--and with the users themselves.[24] The combination of these trends is an exciting process--in many ways fulfilling the vision of the library instruction pioneers--but also brings stress, since it affects what might be called the "meme of self" as librarians struggle to redefine their roles.

Other Memes, Other Models

> Librarians have perhaps not yet fully grasped the extent to which advanced technology and expanding needs and markets are changing that part of the information world they once dominated but which they now have to share with an increasing number and variety of information vendors. As the information world grows, the relative influence of traditional libraries diminishes. It is hard for librarians to accept this.[25]

The preceding discussion has concentrated on the library as the locus for competing ideas, structures, and models. However, libraries are only a part of the information universe. First with the growth of commercial information services, then with the overall computerization of society and the spectacular growth of the Internet, new memes are emerging in which information access is disintermediated and "end users" bypass the library entirely. The World Wide Web, with an eightfold growth in users in 1995, is becoming the primary on-line service for many.[26] The meme of web access is particularly powerful because it is self-reinforcing: a new or improved "browser" program can be announced on the web, and downloaded by thousands of users within a few hours.

Perhaps emblematic of this change is the fact that one of the most widely used information services on the World Wide Web is called "Yahoo!" A term more alien to traditional librarianship, in tone as well as punctuation, could hardly be imagined. This is not to disparage the service in any way, however; it is appropriate for its medium, and it works well for some purposes. Yahoo! does not identify itself with the traditional library meme, but its boldly stated mission stakes a claim on some familiar territory: "To be the world's best guide for information and on-line discovery."[27] As of December 1995, Yahoo! was being accessed by more than 800,000 users a day.[28]

How will the meme of the library fare in this new and expanded infosphere, where people vote with their mice? It is encouraging to note that one of Yahoo!'s key staff members has library training.[29] Librarians from more conventional settings have been very active on the World Wide Web, not only establishing hundreds of institutional sites but also creating resources for universal access, such as the Internet Public Library, OCLC's Internet Cataloging Project, and the University of Michigan's Subject-Oriented Internet Resource Guides.[30] Librarians, often in cooperation with computer scientists, psychologists, and subject-matter experts, are doing increasingly sophisticated development work, as evidenced by the first two Digital Libraries conferences and the NSF/ARPA/NASA Digital Libraries Initiative.[31] Librarians are taking a major role in the search for new paradigms for scholarly communication, through electronic publishing projects such as CORE, MUSE, and TULIP, and the work of groups such as ARL's Office of Scientific and Academic Publishing and the Coalition for Networked Information.[32] The quality of these efforts and others like them may be as important as the intrinsic value of the printed book in ensuring the library's role in the emerging new meme of global information access.

Conclusion

As technology advances, new forms will appear and the proportion of books to film, tapes, disks, and other media will change but the function of the library will continue. Libraries cannot exist without librarians and librarians cannot exist without libraries. The names may change in the future, but their functions will continue as long as there are users who need to gain access to the record in whatever form it takes and wherever it is located.[33]

Ideas--memes--have a life of their own. They live through us, being born as a result of human creativity, replicating and competing for attention in our minds and media, combining with or separating from other memes, and evolving in response to changing conditions. The changing concept of the research library is a classic example of this evolutionary process.

As the quotes interspersed throughout this paper remind us, Richard De Gennaro has contributed significantly to this evolution, helping define and refine the now-dominant meme of the electronically-enhanced, globally-networked, access-oriented library. As Charles Osburn summed it up, "De Gennaro has managed to synthesize large scale, complex situations before they divulged their full evidence to most of the profession, so that his statements helped mold thinking in a way almost unique in our profession. Consistently, he has distinguished the real issues from the perceived issues, brought them into focus, and rendered them productively debatable."[34]

This ability to clarify and evaluate contending ideas has been a key element in De Gennaro's influence. Although he has predicted a number of significant developments, and often been a forceful advocate, his role has not been that of the wild-eyed visionary, but rather that of the incisive analyst, filtering out those memes that would not pass the test of practical experience and common sense. As Russell Shank put it, "His generalizations ... have the appeal of the real."[35]

Notes

1. For links to the Internet sites mentioned in this paper, see the author's home page <http://www.greatbasin.net/~jkup >.

2. De Gennaro, Richard. "Shifting Gears: Information Technology and the Academic Library." *Library Journal* 109 (June 15, 1984): 1204-1209.

3. Vajk, Peter. "Memetics: The Nascent Science of Ideas and Their Transmission." An Essay Presented to the Outlook Club. Berkeley, California, January 19, 1989. <http://www.uio.no/~mwatz/memetics/memetics.txt >. Glenn Grant defines some relevant terms in his "Memetic Lexicon" <http://pespmc1.vub.ac.be/MEMLEX.html >. For a useful list of references, see the alt.memetics newsgroup's FAQ file, "Sources of Infection" < http://www-asds.doc.ic.ac.uk/~ofr/mimetics2.html >.

4. James, William. "Great Men, Great Thoughts, and the Environment." *Atlantic Monthly* 45 (October 1880): 441-459. A version of this text, which varies from the original at least in its title, has been placed on the Internet < http://www.physics.wisc.edu/~shalizi/James/great_men.html >. See also Richards, Robert J. *Darwin and the Emergence of Evolutionary Theories of Mind and Behavior.* Chicago: University of Chicago Press, 1987.

5. Dawkins, Richard. *The Selfish Gene.* New York and Oxford: Oxford University Press, 1976. p. 206. Dawkins was careful to point out that meme rhymes with cream.

6. For a history of this meme, see Rowell, Galen. "Earthscapes from Space." *Outdoor Photographer,* 11 (June 1995): 22-25.

7. See also Henson, Keith. "Memetics: The Science of Information Viruses." *Whole Earth Review,* 57 (Winter 1987): 50-55.

8. Dennett, Daniel C. "Memes and the Exploitation of Imagination." *Journal of Aesthetics and Art Criticism* 48 (Spring 1990): 127-135. This engaging and perceptive account is highly recommended as an introduction to memetics. Hofstadter, Douglas R. "On Viral Sentences and Self-Replicating Structures." *Scientific American,* January 1983; reprinted in *Metamagical Themas: Questing for the Essence of Mind and Pattern.* New York: Basic Books, 1985. pp. 49-64.

9. Dawkins, pp. 211-212.

10. See also Heylighen, Francis. "Memetic Selection Criteria" <http://pespmc1.vub.ac.be/MEMSELC.html >.

11. Dennett, p. 128.

12. De Gennaro, Richard. "Libraries, Technology, and the Information Marketplace." *Library Journal,* 107 (June 1, 1982): 1045-1054.

13. Drabenstott, Karen M. *Analytical Review of the Library of the Future.* Washington: Council on Library Resources, 1993. < ftp://sils.umich.edu/pub/papers/CLR >.

14. De Gennaro, Richard. "Technology and Access in an Enterprise Society." *Library Journal* 114 (October 1, 1989): 40-43.

15. Billings, Harold. "The Bionic Library." *Library Journal* (October 15, 1991): 38-42.

16. De Gennaro, "Shifting Gears," p. 1205.

17. De Gennaro, "Technology and Access in an Enterprise Society," p. 43.

18. Peters, Thomas J. and Robert H. Waterman, Jr. *In Search of Excellence: Lessons from America's Best-run Companies.* New York: Warner Books, 1983; Peters, Thomas J. *Thriving on Chaos: Handbook for a Management Revolution.* New York: Knopf, 1987.

19. Caputo, Janette S. *Stress and Burnout in Library Service.* Phoenix: Oryx Press, 1991; Kupersmith, John. "Technostress in the Bionic Library." *Recreating the Academic Library.* Edited by Cheryl LaGuardia. New York: Neal-Schuman, forthcoming in 1998;"Technostress and the Reference Librarian." *Reference Services Review* 20 (Summer 1992): 7-14, 50.

20. Mitchell, Caroline A. "The CLR Academic Library Management Intern Program." *Library Administration & Management* 6 (Winter 1992): 29-35; Council on Library Resources <http://www-clr.stanford.edu/clr/index.html >.

21. ARL Office of Management Services < http://arl.cni.org/training/basicOMS.html >.

22. De Gennaro, Richard. "Theory vs. Practice in Library Management." *Library Journal,* 108 (July 1983): 1318-1321.

23. For a recent instance, see the "Is Traditional Reference Service Obsolete?" symposium which appeared in *Journal of Academic Librarianship,* 21 (January 1995). This genre, which JAL has used effectively over the years, is a classic example of structured meme competition.

24. Dillon, Dennis. "An Internet Experience: Electronic Information Training Program at the University of Texas." *Library Issues,* 14 (May 1994): 1-4; Kupersmith, John. "Teaching, Learning, and Technostress." *The Upside of Downsizing: Using Library Instruction to Cope.* Edited by Cheryl LaGuardia. New York: Neal-Schuman, 1995. pp. 171-181.

25. De Gennaro, Richard. "Research Libraries Enter the Information Age." *Library Journal* 104 (November 15, 1979): 2405-2410.

26. "Exodus from Commercial Services?" EDUPAGE (January 18, 1996) <http://educom.edu/web/edupage.html >; adapted from *Wall Street Journal* (January 18, 1996): A6.

27. Yahoo! Corporation. "Corporate Fact Sheet" < http://www.yahoo.com/docs/pr/coinfo.html >; see also "Yahoo! History" < http://www.yahoo.com/docs/pr/history.html >.

28. Yahoo! Corporation. "Yahoo! (TM) and Ziff-Davis Establish Web-Driven Publishing Model." Press release (December 12, 1995) < http://www.yahoo.com/docs/pr/release10.html >.

29. Srinija Srinivasan is so described in "The Net 50." *Newsweek* (December 25, 1995/January 1, 1996): 42.

30. Internet Public Library < http://ipl.sils.umich.edu/ >; OCLC Internet Cataloging Project <http://www.oclc.org:6990/ >; University of Michigan's Subject-Oriented Internet Resource Guides < http://www.lib.umich.edu/chhome.html >.

31. Digital Libraries '94: First Annual Conference on the Theory and Practice of Digital Libraries, June 19-21, 1994, College Station, TX < http://www.csdl.tamu.edu/DL94/ >; Digital Libraries '95: Second Annual Conference on the Theory and Practice of Digital Libraries, June 11-13, 1995, Austin, TX < http://www.csdl.tamu.edu/DL95/ >; Digital Libraries Initiative homepage <http://www.grainger.uiuc.edu/dli/national.htm > and press release <http://www.grainger.uiuc.edu/dli/release.htm >.

32. CORE < http://www.oclc.org:5046/projects/core/ >; MUSE < http://muse.jhu.edu/ >; TULIP <http://www.elsevier.nl/info/projects/tulip.htm >; ARL Office of Scientific and Academic Publishing < http://arl.cni.org/scomm/scomm.html >; Coalition for Networked Information <http://www.cni.org/CNI.homepage.html >.

33. De Gennaro, "Libraries, Technology, and the Information Marketplace," p. 1049.

34. Osburn, Charles B. Review of *Libraries, Technology, and the Information Marketplace: Selected Papers* by Richard De Gennaro, *Library Resources and Technical Services* 32 (April 1988), 189.

35. Shank, Russell. Review of *Libraries, Technology, and the Information Marketplace: Selected Papers* by Richard De Gennaro, *Journal of Academic Librarianship* 14 (July 1988), 168-170.

Cooperation: Not the Only Nor Always the Best Solution

by Maurice B. Line

Cooperation has always been assumed to be a good thing and has been a key theme of many conferences. But much thinking has focused on the means of cooperation rather than on the ends that cooperation is intended to serve and neglected to fully explore other means of attaining those ends. Cooperative schemes have rarely been subjected to rigorous cost-effectiveness analysis; most have been national or subnational rather than international; and some areas where cooperation could be useful have received little attention. Cooperation on a goodwill basis is already giving way to commercial arrangements between libraries as well as with private suppliers. The growth of private providers of various services and the ability of information technology to transcend geographical boundaries are two factors among several that make a radical reappraisal of cooperation increasingly necessary.

Introduction

Cooperation has always been a popular issue among librarians. It figures on the agenda of conference after conference. Attempt after attempt has been made to establish cooperative schemes for the sharing of bibliographic records, access to the holdings of libraries, and shared acquisition programs. "We must cooperate or die" is a constant refrain. "If we don't cook up a cooperative scheme we can't be doing our job" might be a better one; put four or five librarians in a room for long enough, and it is odds-on that they will generate a cooperative scheme. Cooperation seems as natural to librarians as nest-building is to birds, scavenging to hyenas, and leaping up waterfalls to salmon.

Richard De Gennaro, a pioneer of library automation and one of our most prominent thinkers and writers, has made notable contributions to the debate, among them a 1975 article on "Austerity, technology and resource sharing" [1] and one of 1980 on "Resource sharing in a network environment" [2] If this paper challenges (as it does) some conventional thinking on cooperation, it is in accord with Dick's constant reminders to librarians that they must adapt to changed conditions and circumstances. Indeed, one of my themes was dealt with by Dick seventeen years ago in his article on "From monopoly to competition" [3]

I recently had occasion to read a large number of reports and papers on cooperation, for a study I was asked to carry out in the UK.[4] My reading led me to several general conclusions:

- The *purposes* which cooperation can serve are often not clearly identified. cooperation is generally accepted as something that exists and that there ought to be more of.
- As a result of this, there is little or no attempt to look at alternative means of serving these purposes.
- There is a lack of clarity as to what cooperation means. It seems to be taken to mean any activity which involves two or more libraries using one another's services or facilities.

- The view of cooperation in many documents is rather narrow; it is largely focused on provision of and access to library materials.
- cooperation is generally viewed from national aspects only; supranational and global aspects are neglected.
- Many writings on cooperative projects claim great improvements over the previous situation. However, since the cost-effectiveness of the prior situation usually was never calculated, even when measures are given for the new situation we cannot make comparisons. And, when even if we could, there is no means of knowing whether similar improvements could have been made for less cost by other means. It goes without saying that failed cooperative projects are never reported; once a scheme is embarked upon, the cooperators (like politicians) have a vested interest in claiming success and suppressing failure.
- There is little attempt to look more than a few years ahead in a realistic manner. To be sure, revolutionary changes as a result of information technology are predicted, but they are often imprecise.

It must first be said that cooperation embraces a vast number of informal transactions. Human beings are generally willing to help one another, within limits, and a great deal of cooperation takes place between librarians every day, in person, by phone, by mail, and in other ways. This is not what we think of when cooperation is mentioned, but it cannot be ignored; it does an immense amount to oil the wheels of library operations, and its value is without question, if only in making everyone's life more livable. However, cooperation is commonly used to mean cooperative schemes, whose value is very much open to question.

It is sometimes said that there is plenty of lip service to cooperation, but little real cooperation in practice. It is doubtful whether this is true, or if it is a matter for criticism. Admittedly, librarians talk about cooperation more than they practise it, but there are few supposed virtuous activities that are not more admired than practised, and libraries have never given up trying to cooperate. The world is littered with cooperative schemes, past and present, and if some of them are defunct or little used it may simply be that they are no longer useful. Libraries probably cooperate as much as they need to and can afford to (in terms of staff and resources). There is no virtue in cooperation in itself; and there are almost certainly more examples of failed or cost-ineffective (cost-defective?) cooperation than there are of cooperative opportunities missed.

The Nature and Scope of Cooperation

Having made these criticisms, I need to state my own position. The working definition of cooperation given in one recent British report [5] is "The creation and operation of equitable, that is mutually 'fair', collaborative arrangements between libraries and information providers which enhance the common good through making information available to all potential users (without obstacle to access by reason of cost) which is more extensive or more valuable to the user and/or is of lower cost to the collaborating providers". Even if the ambiguity of "between libraries and information providers" is ignored, this seems unsatisfactory, since it implies that cooperation is by definition always beneficial; but cooperation can be good, bad or neutral - it does not have to be "more extensive or more valuable" or "of lower cost" in order to constitute cooperation

The term cooperation seems to me to mean transactions or arrangements between bodies that have an element of goodwill and mutuality. This definition excludes some activities commonly regarded as cooperative. The use of commonly available resources for payment is not cooperation. The use of privately owned services, public services run on a fully commercial basis (including transactions between libraries on such a basis), or centrally available services such as the British Library Document Supply Centre (BLDSC), is not cooperation, even though it may require agreements on procedures. The same applies to OCLC, often held up as a shining example of cooperation; in fact, the only cooperation that takes place now is that there is consultation on the systems used; the day to day use of the system is not organized at all. Transactions between libraries for which costs are partially recovered do involve cooperation.

There can also be *collaboration* between organizations and systems that do not otherwise cooperate and that operate on a commercial basis; e.g. they may agree to avoid deliberate competition with one another, or divide up the territory between them, or agree on a single pricing system. In the UK, BLDSC and the regional library systems, which are largely public library-based, collaborate quite closely now, though there can be no question that BLDSC has over the last 30 years taken a very large proportion of the demand that would otherwise have gone through the regional systems (as well as a great volume of demand that would not have been made at all because the systems could not have coped).

Some systems that started off as cooperative have gradually turned into commercial activities; OCLC is a prime example. We are moving away from the world of cooperation towards a world of partnerships, alliances, etc. Some of these may be temporary and very limited; whereas in cooperation some degree of permanence has generally been aimed at.

The *aim* of library cooperation is surely the same as that of libraries in general: to ensure that library and information resources are used as fully and cost-effectively as possible to provide all citizens with equal access to library materials and information. If it does not serve this purpose, or if it does not do so any better (more effectively, more efficiently) than would happen without cooperation, there is no point in it.

It should be noted that the priorities of cooperative efforts that originated in a spirit of service and later became commercial have changed; at the least they aim to keep their economic heads above water and at best to make a profit. That does not mean of course that they provide a worse service; indeed, they are likely to provide a better one, since their survival (unlike that of cooperatives) depends on the service they give.

Apart from going it alone, which no library can now contemplate, many of the purposes served by cooperation can be partly or wholly served by commercial bodies, and indeed are being so served; and if cooperation is defined in the narrower sense above, some transactions between libraries as well as between them and commercial bodies can take place on a purely commercial basis.

Cooperation can involve shared ownership of a facility - e.g. a deacidification centre - which is jointly funded and accessible to all members, or mutual use of resources held by a number of libraries. To these might be added agreed systems or procedures, e.g. for interlending. Much interlending involves both the second and third. Agreed procedures may exist where there is no other form of cooperation, e.g. interlending could take place on a purely commercial basis but for the convenience of all participants may agree on a system of common charges and protocols.

Cooperation can take a great variety of forms. These include:
- acquisition of material
- production of and access to bibliographic records
- access to material
- disposal of material
- consultation of library collections
- information provision
- training
- sharing of equipment for conservation
- microfilming programmes.

All these types of cooperation can serve the aim as defined above, for example, by preserving older material and thus making it accessible, by enabling staff to serve people more effectively, and so on. The aforementioned report [5] distinguishes "between forms of cooperation which directly affect the services available to users, such as inter-lending, and forms of cooperation which improve the capabilities of libraries and information services to meet their users" needs, such as the development of occupational competence standards...". It does not, however, cover many kinds of cooperation.

Cooperation can take place on various scales: local (over small areas), subnational (e.g. states in the case of the USA), national, supranational (covering areas of the world such as Western Europe), or global. Within each area, it can be sectoral - by type of library, by subject area, by type of material (e.g. sound recordings) or by type of client. Now that electronic technology is overcoming the tyranny of distance, it makes little sense to discuss many kinds of cooperation purely in a national or subnational context.

Not only is there no virtue in cooperation *per se*, but there can be drawbacks. Cooperation, as we are often reminded, costs money; it may save money in the long run, but the run often turns out to be a marathon. The organization of cooperative schemes can present formidable logistic problems, especially in the case of cooperative acquisition schemes. Formal schemes can lock libraries into systems and procedures that are hard to change when they need to be changed and, by freezing processes at a certain point, can inhibit desirable developments and valuable innovations.

Factors Affecting the Future of Cooperation

Many of the factors that are affecting libraries generally are relevant - some of them especially relevant - to cooperation. The impact of information technology is obviously a massive one. Academic and other research libraries are largely networked already; public libraries lag some way behind. (In the UK in 1995, while 53% of public library systems had an Internet connection, only 3% of individual service points were wired up.) The Internet, which is a disorganized system if ever there was one, will change things in unknown ways; one main way is by breaking down geographical boundaries.

Some kinds of media (e.g. CD-ROMs) cannot normally be lent because of restrictions imposed by the producers. It is technically possible to transmit some kinds of material (e.g. sound and video recordings) electronically. The increasing use of electronic media for text will have a profound impact on all document access and supply. The direct access by the consumer that electronic storage and access make possible will have a profound impact.

There is a general trend towards decentralization. In several unitary as well as federal nations more regional devolution is being demanded. This appears to be largely based both on a realization (not least in industry) that concentration of power and control in one place is inefficient and on a vaguer but increasingly widespread distrust of central control. People as well as countries may want to share, but they also want to be free to do their own thing. If there is a high degree of decentralization, it has to be decided what (if anything) needs to be done nationally.

Reduced library funding is a universal problem, which is unlikely to go away. It affects cooperation in both negative and positive ways: it forces libraries to look after their own interests more - to be more selfish; but it also makes them look towards cooperative ways of reducing the financial strain.

Another major trend, strongly influenced by technology, is that the boundaries of library operations and services are becoming much less clear: the borders between publishers, information brokers and libraries are breaking down. There is also an increasing trend towards convergence in academic institutions between libraries, computing and learning resource departments - and perhaps in local authorities between libraries and other cultural activities.

The shift from holdings to access is well documented, and embraced by some librarians with surprising enthusiasm [6] However, I believe that the shift is smaller and slower than might be thought from reading the literature, that it is made unwillingly in many cases, and that it is not necessarily desirable in principle.[7]

The trend towards globalization is worldwide and unstoppable. There is a clear need, more apparent in Europe than in the USA, for libraries to think in terms of larger geographical and political groupings.

There is also a trend, driven by economic reality as well as political ideology, to put activities of many kinds that used to be free on a more commercial basis. What this means is that the cost is borne by the customer rather than the supplier. A distinction needs to be made between charging individual users and charging other libraries for services rendered. Goodwill is giving way, as a matter of principle as well as practice, to cost recovery.

The private information sector is doing quite a few things that libraries used to do, including the supply of catalogue records and journal articles. This offers libraries as customers a choice of suppliers; but if libraries as suppliers offer similar services to the private sector they may undercut them unfairly. Very few private suppliers are regional; many are international.

All these trends and factors together necessitate a fresh look at cooperation as well as other activities. Some, like reductions in library budgets, are commonly thought to favour cooperation - a belief that I question.

Planning

In many countries, though not so much in the USA, national planning or action is thought to be needed for cooperation, in particular, for creating a national network infrastructure, spanning all types of library, and a framework for cooperation of various kinds, especially document access, within which local, sectoral, regional and national schemes can operate without unnecessary duplication of effort and expenditure of money.

There have been regular pleas over the years for planning, preferably on the national level. Many of these have essentially been pleas for national funding. Others seem to arise from inertia or a sense of helplessness - that nothing can be done without central planning or support. Pleas for bodies with teeth (which would be used solely to bite others) seem to have died out, in favour of consensus planning. There is some feeling that regions should prepare plans which could guide or lead to national plans. It is hard however to find a well argued and convincing case for a national strategy, which states clearly what one would actually do.

De facto national policy is common. In most countries, governments can and do have a huge influence on what happens to libraries, nationally and individually, by their allocation of funds; for example, if it was decided in the UK to reduce (even) more dramatically the grant-in-aid to the British Library, other libraries would have to play a larger role in national bibliographic and document supply services. If at the same time the government made special funds available to academic libraries to fill the gap, the effect would be even greater. This may be an extreme example, but government policies and decisions have had similar large effects in the past - the most obvious being the setting up of the National Lending Library for Science and Technology in the early 1960s and the British Library a decade later. It is impossible now to say how far such decisions were part of an unspoken national policy and how far reactions to specific needs and problems - more probably the latter than the former. Whatever strategies are developed for the future, they can easily be upset by the imposition of financial restrictions.

Planning, more specifically strategic planning, is a characteristic of many formal schemes. There has been a reaction against strategic planning in recent years [8] on the grounds that it is impossible to see more than one or two years ahead and that the attempt to plan ahead inhibits flexibility and reduces the capacity to respond to new circumstances. Several less developed countries have produced National Information Plans, which are out of date as soon as they are written but which may direct policy for years ahead. Fortunately, most strategic plans for three years or more are in fact largely ignored after the first year; all that is lost is the goodwill and trust of the staff who have invested time and effort in it. What is needed is rather a different kind of plan, consisting of a statement of general objectives, a vision of where the organization or cooperative system wants to be in ten years" time, and short term strategies to move towards the vision and objectives. The process is more important than the plan.

Most individual cooperative schemes are carefully planned and managed. However, if one looks at the systems within which most day to day transactions across and between libraries take place, they are either unplanned or involve minimal planning and organization, on the part of those using them: the Internet, OCLC, BLDSC. This phenomenon is not confined to librarianship: many schemes of all kinds are over-organized by those whose tidy minds are offended by apparent disorder. Moreover, most of the best innovations are not the product of planning on the part of any national or other body, but of individual innovators, people like Frederick Kilgour and Donald Urquhart. Would any planning committee have come up with OCLC or the National Lending Library for Science and Technology (now the British Library Document Supply Centre)? It is of course possible for cooperative schemes to originate in the inspiration of individuals, as OCLC did. Some other good cooperative schemes seem to have evolved, with no obvious planning (and also with no premature or excessive claims of success).

Awareness of local, regional and national resources is essential; but this can be achieved without formal schemes or plans. For the holdings of libraries, this is happening anyway with more and more catalogues accessible online. For subject expertise there are several national and other guides, and more may be desirable.

The above is not intended as an attack on planning; rather, it is a criticism of elaborate and unrealistic planning and, especially, of national plans. What *is* needed is the collection and national availability of information on cooperation and other joint arrangements: what schemes exist, what libraries are involved and what each scheme aims to do; how well they perform, from their inception and year by year, in as much detail as possible, preferably using standard measures presented in a standard form. This is, incidentally, one area where cooperation is necessary - unless compulsion were to be used for the collection of information (if it were it would almost certainly not work).

Cooperative Acquisition

Dr. Johnson said of a man who had a very unhappy relationship with his first wife that his second marriage represented the triumph of hope over experience. The same could be said of cooperative acquisition schemes. The temptation is obvious. What more natural for libraries with acquisition budgets under pressure than to share acquisition programs? Yet although many such schemes have been tried, few have succeeded.

There are excellent reasons why this might have been expected. If the aim is to acquire material that could not, or would not, be acquired by any one library for its own clients, that means that the libraries involved are expected to acquire materials they do not need in the prospect that some other library in the system may need them. This requires either a great deal of money or a rare degree of altruism, since while they are doing this they may be failing to acquire materials that their clients do want. And who is to say what extra materials they should acquire? What kind of materials are they? Materials that are thought worthy of a large library collection? Worthy on what grounds? Of their likelihood of being wanted in future? But who can predict that? Who is to say that libraries in cooperative schemes are not acquiring items that are never ever wanted? Some articles on cooperative schemes justify their success on the grounds that the total number of titles acquired among the cooperating libraries has much increased; but this is of no importance if the extra titles are never used. Materials that are wanted today are more likely to be wanted tomorrow than materials that are not wanted today.

It is rather invidious to take specific examples, but great success is claimed for VIVA (Virtual Library of Virginia) in a recent paper [9] "There has been a dramatic cost savings, with the group sometimes paying as little as 13% of what the cost of access would have been had each institution purchased the resource separately." What precisely is included in the cost of access is not stated in the report (which is no more than the summary of a presented paper). The speaker herself pointed out that "each of the resources would not have been purchased if left up to the individual institutions" and also expressed concern that "VIVA members could face permanent budget reductions if the extent of the savings were publicized too heavily". This danger could almost certainly be averted if the scheme were fully costed, since members may well have acquired as part of the scheme material that was not wanted. On the other hand, the danger could be increased if a comparison were made with the cost of getting the material from more remote sources. The speaker also mentioned various obstacles and concluded that "cooperation works, but it takes a lot of work to cooperate".

Even preparing a cooperative acquisition policy can be difficult, if it involves the agreement of numerous bodies, as it usually does; and to put a policy into practice has proved almost impossible, except by building up central resources such as BLDSC. Co-operative national provision has been tried numerous times in numerous countries, even across countries; the best known and most ambitious example is the Scandia Plan.[10] The attempts have consumed vast quantities of money and time - to such little effect that many schemes have been abandoned, defeated by a shortage of resources and by logistics. If a shortage of money makes cooperative acquisition difficult at a national level, it makes it no easier at a subnational (state or regional) level; and if logistics are a problem at the national level, they are still more of a problem at the supranational level.

The concept of the Distributed National Collection has had much currency in the last five or six years in Australia [11] largely as a result of severe reductions in the funding of the National Library of Australia; the Australians have tried to make a virtue of necessity. The principle is that maintaining a national collection should not (and cannot) be the responsibility of any one library; in practice, it is argued, electronic technology makes this objective much easier to achieve. Access to the nation's library resources is an obvious objective, well on its way to being achieved as the holdings of more and more libraries become accessible on-line. The question is whether it makes much sense to deliberately plan a national collection when access to information resources, like much else, is being globalized.[12]

It is true that electronic technology makes cooperative schemes easier to manage, since the holdings and order lists of libraries in a system can be readily accessed. But at the same time electronic technology makes national acquisition schemes increasingly unnecessary for copiable materials (e.g. articles from serials), and of diminishing value for non-copiable ones (mainly monographs).

It is questionable if any planning would achieve much even if it were possible to put into practice. If individual libraries acquire a reasonable number of items each year and if these are accessible, no scheme can really add much; while if libraries cannot afford to acquire many items, cooperative planning becomes even less possible.

Information access, like so many other things, is becoming globalized. It is still rather cheaper and quicker to borrow books from within most countries than from other countries, but the difference is diminishing; British libraries sometimes find it quicker and easier to borrow a book from a U.S. library via OCLC than to use the British cooperative system. As for periodicals, the barrier of distance is disappearing altogether. Why then, it may be asked, do libraries persist in developing local, subnational and national cooperative acquisition schemes? One answer is that if libraries are fairly close together it is possible to visit them and consult collections at first hand. This, however, is an argument for a single large library in each area or region, not for a number of medium-sized libraries sharing acquisitions. The exception is libraries that specialize in a particular field; but they presumably specialize anyway, scheme or no scheme, and they are very unevenly distributed around the country.

When the Conspectus first came on the library scene, it was hailed as a tool for improving cooperative acquisition. Quite apart from the question of the value of cooperative acquisition, the Conspectus seems to me a splendid example of librarians' ingenuity in creating a tool that requires a great deal of time and effort to use, produces information that is very rarely comparable between libraries, and hardly ever results in any useful action. It seems to have almost disappeared from the literature recently, not, I suspect, because it has become accepted but because it has been largely abandoned - after how much expenditure?

My earlier comments on the failure to evaluate are especially valid in the case of cooperative acquisition schemes. A proper evaluation would first calculate costs and the availability and use of wanted items before the scheme started and again when the scheme had been running for, say, three years, six years, and so on. The additional benefits, if any, would be measured against the additional costs. Admittedly, a full detailed cost-benefit evaluation is rarely possible, but that does not mean that the attempt should not be made; and, in many cases, a rough evaluation would provide sufficient answers. It would constitute a great advance if standard measures could be agreed upon for use in comparative evaluation.

Cooperative Retention and Preservation

One area where cooperation *is* desirable is the retention of materials in research libraries. It is clearly important that significant, and perhaps unique, material should not be lost to the country (and perhaps to other countries as well). There is little if any point in doing this on any smaller scale than a national one, yet few countries have national retention plans. Fortunately, there is some cooperation in the expensive activity of microfilming materials, mainly in the form of registers of microform masters, which help to avoid duplication of effort.

Allied to retention is preservation. Here again cooperation is desirable in such forms as a shared deacidification plant. But, as noted earlier, this constitutes cooperation only if the plant is commonly owned. If it is owned by one institution and used by others, presumably for payment (since it is hard to see any other basis for use), it is not cooperation but a commercial transaction.

Cooperative Remote Access

Effective access within and between countries requires: the general agreement of libraries involved to supply materials; the construction and maintenance of files of records (i.e. union lists); and mechanisms for requesting and supply (e.g. standard procedures and forms). Even the second is not always necessary, since it is possible for several catalogues to be put up on the same system and searched as if they were one. Arrangements for access used to be almost solely a matter for libraries, but there are now a considerable number of private suppliers who supply libraries for payment (not on a cooperative basis).

One major reason why document supply between libraries is not always very efficient is that libraries are under no obligation other than a moral one to supply other libraries; and morals have had to give way in several countries to financial realities as heavy net suppliers are simply unable to give a decent service free. The situation is better in the UK than in most other countries largely because the great bulk of demand is met by BLDSC and because most marginal costs are recovered if BLDSC forms are used between libraries as well as for requests to BLDSC. The question of whether full costs should be recovered will inevitably have to be faced soon in all countries. This would put interlibrary document supply on the same basis as commercial document supply, reducing the cooperative element to agreed protocols and procedures and, perhaps, standard charges.

Efforts to improve remote access should focus a number of areas. There should be a concentration on the development of records with sufficient standardization to make searches in different catalogues simple, and interfiling possible. There is a need for the development protocols for standard requesting and supply procedures. There should be concern for networked national access to catalogues and standard charges (already largely there). There needs to be within this process an acceptance by libraries that they have some obligation to supply materials to other libraries (this should not be difficult, since if they do not they will not be able to request any).

Access for Consultation

In the U.K. there has been concern over the apparent excessive use of some libraries, both public and academic, by alien students. The evidence of this excessive use is rather thin, and that it imposes any strain or cost on the libraries affected is thinner still. But supposing that it is a problem, the solution is not for the libraries to ban students but to make a contract for payment by their institutions. This is, in fact, suggested by one of the British reports [13], though cautiously, as a possibility to be studied; the study would include a more detailed estimate of the alien demand and of the costs incurred.

Charging

What emerges from the foregoing discussion is first that all cooperative exercises should be properly costed and otherwise evaluated and second that costs should be recovered. Cooperation is already giving way to commercial arrangements, for several reasons. There is a general political and public reaction against things that are free. Demands for services that local libraries cannot provide are growing and putting strain on the system. Commercial suppliers are playing an increasingly larger role, both in serving people directly and in serving libraries. Libraries are being forced to charge one another for services and are likely to move towards full cost recovery. Finally, short-term alliances and partnerships, between different libraries and between libraries and commercial providers, are becoming more common.

The debate over charging, which has been a hot one in many countries, especially in Scandinavia, has often confused charging individual users and charging customer libraries. There is a case for charging individuals for some non-basic (value-added) services, but it is a separate one, with which I am not concerned here.

Charging customer libraries is desirable for most services and vital for regular expensive services. There is no conceivable reason why providers should bear the cost. Free and subsidized arrangements are liable to suffer when budgets and staff numbers decline; charges are necessary if some services are to be introduced or improved, or perhaps to survive at all. Providers should not only be able to provide if they are properly paid; they are under an obligation to do so. Customer libraries should, in their own interest, have to calculate the cost-efficiency balance between providing a service themselves and buying it from elsewhere; otherwise there is little logical reason why they should not depend on other libraries for everything. Further, free provision undercuts commercial providers.

One commonly used argument against charging is that it can cost more to charge than to give a service free and that most libraries are roughly in balance with one another. The latter is rarely true; few libraries are in balance with another library in the provision of any service. As for the cost of charging, this can be very small if systems of payment are used that do not require an invoice to be raised for every transaction; it is often possible to use average costs (which tend to even out if demand is fairly high) rather than carefully calculated differential costs. This is not always possible, and there are cases where charging is pointless; the principle of relative cost-effectiveness should be applied to charging as to other matters.

Another argument against charging is that rich libraries have a duty to help poor ones. But apart from the doubtful wisdom of regarding libraries in the same way as charitable individuals, free services do not in the end help the customer library; as indicated above, they conceal the fact that it is inadequately funded, and its parent body, therefore, has no reason or incentive to increase its support.

A contractual paid basis is a much sounder foundation for most interlibrary services than free cooperative arrangements. When a service is put on a contractual paid basis it ceases to be cooperation. This is not a cause for lamentation; on such a basis useless schemes are quickly weeded out, and those that are necessary and valued survive.

Conclusions

This paper is not so much an attack on present cooperative systems (though there is some of that in it) as an attempt to take a fresh look at the nature, aims and desirability of cooperation in the hope that it might encourage others to pursue the argument and think through the implications for the future of library and information services. No doubt some cooperative schemes do achieve valuable results. Cooperative cataloguing, for example, is here to stay, though that may become even more of a commercial activity than it is already. The trouble is that it is very hard to know which do achieve results and which do not. Unless they are on a commercial basis and made subject to economic realities, schemes that are not cost-beneficial may have unnecessarily prolonged lives. However, the more commercial they are, the less cooperative they become.

My general conclusions can be summarized as follow:

- Cooperation implies some degree of mutuality; access to widely available resources is not necessarily cooperation.
- There is a great variety of cooperative schemes, some of which - perhaps many - are of dubious current value, whatever their value may have been in the past. Many, if not most, of them are in need of a radical scrutiny.
- External funding for schemes on any scale cannot be expected; the most that can be hoped for is support for pilot experimental systems that look likely to yield economies or benefits if adopted on a wider scale.
- Cooperative grace and favour arrangements are giving way to commercial-type arrangements, including formal contracts. In the future, there are likely to be numerous partnerships, temporary or longer-lived, mostly on a contractual basis between libraries and other information bodies that fall outside the scope of cooperation as understood in the past. Since this is a process that cannot be halted, it is sensible to embrace it and make future arrangements on this basis rather than to try to resist it and keep cooperative procedures in place as long as possible.

- The supply of and access to documents and bibliographic records are now national and international matters, and there is less need to think in terms of provision within countries.
- The need for remote access to documents should focus *at a national level* on (a) records with sufficient standardization to make searches in different catalogues simple and interfiling possible, (b) standard requesting and supply procedures and protocols, (c) standard charges, (d) networked national access to catalogues, and (e) an acceptance by libraries that they have some obligation to supply materials to other libraries (this ought not to be difficult, since if they do not they will not be in a good position to request any).
- Access to libraries for purposes of consultation access should be offered as a general principle, and based on financial agreements if these prove desirable in economic terms.
- No amount of cooperative or other joint activity, and no currently conceivable developments in electronic technology, can serve as a full substitute for adequate local libraries. If the relative decline in library funding continues, it will inevitably restrict access to information and knowledge.
- Other forms of joint activity than the customary ones of document and bibliographic access deserve more attention. Some of these may need initial funds (government or borrowed) to get them started, but they can then be put on a commercial basis (e.g. use of conservation facilities such as deacidification chambers).
- There is little need for national planning, except to create the technological infrastructure for information access and use.
- National action on cooperative and other joint enterprises is needed, however, to establish, as far as possible on a consensual basis, principles and standards for costing and charging, to collect and share information on activities, to establish performance measures for cooperative and other joint enterprises, and to monitor them regularly for effectiveness and efficiency.

Finally, I would like to suggest a few principles of cooperation:
- Cooperation must serve a clearly defined purpose; it has no virtue in itself.
- Other means of achieving any desired objective should be explored.
- The justification of any means chosen must lie in its cost-effectiveness.
- Cooperation should not be undertaken unless it is likely to produce better results than would be achieved by other means.
- Cooperation should be looked at in a global context.
- Over-planning should be avoided, and top-down planning is almost always undesirable.

In a rapidly changing world, not only may the old answers no longer suffice, but also the questions may be changing. I have little doubt that Dick De Gennaro would agree with me that, together with many of the things that libraries do, cooperation, that long-treasured solution, needs a thorough reassessment.

Notes

1. De Gennaro, Richard. "Austerity, Technology, and Resource Sharing: Research Libraries Face the Future." *Library Journal,* (15 May 1975) 917-923.

2. De Gennaro, Richard. "Resource Sharing in a Network Environment." *Library Journal,* (1 February 1980) 353-355.

3. De Gennaro, Richard "From Monopoly to Competition: The Changing Library Network Scene." *Library Journal,* (1 June 1979) 1215-1217.

4. Line, Maurice B. *The Future of Library and Information Cooperation in the UK and Ireland: an Independent Assessment.* Report for the [UK] Library and Information Cooperation Council. 1996.

5. APT Partnership. *The APT Review: A Review of Library and Information Cooperation in the UK and Republic of Ireland.* For the Library and Information Cooperation Council (LINC). Sheffield: LINC, 1995. (BL R&D Report 6212).

6. Widdicombe, Richard P. "Eliminating All Journal Subscriptions has Freed our Customers to Seek Information They Really Want and Need: the Result - More Access, Not Less." *Science and Technology Libraries* 14:1, Fall 1993: 3-13.

7. Line, Maurice B. "Access Versus Ownership: How Real an Alternative is It?" *IFLA Journal* 22:2 1996: 35-41.

8. Mintzberg, Henry. "The Fall and Rise of Strategic Planning." *Harvard Business Review* 72:1 January/February 1994: 107-114.

9. "Cooperation Works! Successful Models of Cooperative Collection Development: Report of a Program". *Library Acquisitions: Practice and Theory,* 20:2 Summer 1996: 190-192.

10. Hannesdóttir, Sigrún Klara. *The Scandia Plan: A Cooperative Acquisition Scheme for Improving Access to Research Publications in Four Nordic Countries.* Metuchen, NJ & London: Scarecrow Press, 1992.

11. Henty, Margaret. "Resource Sharing Ideals and Realities: The Case of Australia's Distributed National Collection." *Advances in Collection Development and Resource Sharing 1.* 1995: 139-152.

12. The arguments are more fully presented in a study I carried out for the Royal Library in the Netherlands last year, and a subsequent paper largely based on it: Line, Maurice B. "International Library Access as an Alternative to National Collection Development in the

Netherlands." *Collecties op Achterstand: Buitenlandse Wetenschappelijke Literatuur in Nederlandse Bibliotheken.* Den Haag: Koninklijke Bibliotheek, 1996. pp.19-35.

13. Line, Maurice B. "National Self-Sufficiency in an Electronic Age;" as it appears in Helal, A.H. and Weiss,-J.W.-(eds.) -*Electronic Documents and Information: From Preservation to Access.* 18th International Essen Symposium, October 1995. Essen: Universitäts-bibliothek, 1996. pp.170-193.

14. Joint Funding Councils' Libraries Review. *Report of a National/Regional Strategy for Library Provision for Researchers* [Chair: Michael Anderson]. Bristol: HEFCE, 1995.

Anticipating the Future from the Successes of the Past

by Susan K. Martin

One of the most important characteristics of a strong leader is the ability to assess the contemporary environment, extrapolate the effects of this environment, and make decisions for the organization based upon a judgment of the future which, to most ordinary people, seems outlandish and unreasonable. In the course of leading his or her institution in this way, at least two events may result: other leaders consider the steps that are being taken and imitate them; and the future is actually changed as the result of the intuition of this leader.

Authors often say, with amusement, that they are comfortable in predicting trends and issues of the future, because no one ever goes back to compare what has been said in the past with the real-life outcome. On this occasion, however, we are celebrating the professional life and work of a statesman of the library profession who has over the years proven himself to be an incisive analyst of contemporary trends and a frequent prognosticator about the issues and problems of the future.

In Richard De Gennaro's book, *Libraries, Technology, and the Information Marketplace*, is a chapter written in 1981, containing the thoughtful heading "Beware of Prediction."[1] Within that paper, De Gennaro tells us that

> "Anyone can enjoy the intellectual sport of speculating about the wonders of information technology in the year 2000 and beyond, but some of us--managers, trustees, entrepreneurs--must try to see and assess the near-term future of that technology and make plans to use it appropriately. I define near-term future as five to ten years ahead; trying to see and plan beyond that is largely guesswork."[2]

After reviewing the papers in De Gennaro's book, this writer was struck by not only the insight of the analyses, but also by the apparent accuracy of his predictions and projections for the future. Therefore, it is useful to evaluate the predictions he made, determine which ones have already been proven to be correct, and examine those that have not yet come to pass, in order to construct a scenario for the library of the future, based on the judgment of a writer whose past prognoses have already been demonstrated to be largely correct. Librarians often seek guidance for their present decisions and actions, hoping that these decisions will be appropriate to the academic, business, and technological world of the future. With a sizable body of predictions that can be identified as largely correct, these librarians should then be able to assess the remaining predictions, make a correction for events that have occurred over the passage of time, and use these predictions to prompt decisions that need to be made today and in the future.

Over the course of more than twenty years, De Gennaro wrote more than forty papers in four areas: information technologies and access to information; libraries and the information marketplace; management of the library in transition; and library automation and networking. With the exception of the very earliest works, which were primarily descriptive in nature, most of his writings were incisive probes of specific contemporary issues with suggestions for current and future action or "trend" papers, in which he analyzed particular topics as they affected libraries over a period of two or even three decades, with projections of these trends as they would influence libraries in the future.

Most of his writings and, therefore, predictions concern academic and research libraries, and reflect the outlook of a leader in several academic settings over the decades. Public schools and special libraries are generally not included in his works; therefore, only the broadest of his predictions would be relevant to these groups of libraries.

One might expect that these predictions would not take into account the impact of events or technologies that did not exist in the 1970s and '80s, when De Gennaro did the bulk of his writing. Among these are the Internet, the Worldwide Web, the very conservative political changes that have affected our entire society in the past decade, and the evolution of technological change at a rate that even Alvin Toffler might not have thought possible.[3] For the most part, indeed, De Gennaro's writing focused more specifically on the research library issues, publishing, and information technology of the time. Some projections have been outpaced by the rapidly changing technologies. However, some of the prognostications are remarkable in their anticipation of an environment that was totally unknown at the time. For example, in 1984, he wrote: "when...microprocessors are linked to large mainframes, optical and digital disk systems, database machines, local area networks, and the various library and commercial information networks, library automation and information automation will converge, and a new wave of synergistic development will take place..."[4] This description sounds very much like the Internet, couched in terms used in the 1980s.

Analysis of the predictions

From the aforementioned book, which contains thirty-nine papers written between 1965 and 1987, this writer identified 155 statements which could be treated as predictions, and then tested for four possible outcomes:

(1)   the prediction was correct, and events have already occurred as suggested;
(2)   the prediction was incorrect; the events did not occur as suggested, and it is already clear that intervening circumstances have superseded the prediction;
(3)   the prediction was partially correct; the current environment does not reflect exactly the terms of the prediction, but the prognostication was not totally incorrect, either. (For example, in 1973, De Gennaro wrote that libraries would not be able to deal with specialized information such as the census, but would

have to rely upon discrete information centers to acquire and process these databases. As we now know, libraries do need to rely upon special information centers to process this information, but they are then able to deal with the resulting product in serving their clienteles); and

(4)   the events described in the prediction have not yet happened, but they have not been made obsolete by the passage of time; therefore, it is still possible that the events could take place.

It is on the fourth category of predictions above that this paper focuses, hoping to extrude from this large body of insights and prognoses those points that can be of use to libraries as they approach the 21st century.

Of the 155 predictions in the four categories, 99 can be determined to have been correct; 21 were incorrect, or were superseded by events; and 13 were partially correct. Twenty-two predictions have not yet come to pass.

The remainder of this paper describes this last group of predictions, examines them within the light of today's technological, academic and political environment, and suggests which issues should be of continuing concern to librarians as they face the future. The rate of success of De Gennaro's predictions indicates that we should look carefully at the predictions of events that have not yet occurred, because it is likely that the majority of them will either transpire more or less as predicted, or will transpire in part as predicted. In either case, the projections should be instructive for library managers as they prepare for the future.

The Library of the Future: Access

Prediction: "The total amount of interlibrary loan and photocopying in lieu of interlibrary loan is and will always remain a relatively small fraction of total library use".(1977)[5] The point of this statement was to suggest that there would always be a need for continuing to strengthen local collections for local use. Interlibrary Loan began as a stepchild of the library operation, and while there has been significant improvement in funding and activity over the years, a look at the statistics of virtually all libraries will show that in-house and local use continue to far overshadow the interlibrary loan -- and document delivery -- operations of the library. Efforts in recent years to share collection development processes, or to share collections themselves, may be successful in a few institutions, but the traditional patterns of use are changing not toward interlibrary library and document delivery, but toward electronic databases and full-text that may be located in-house or on the Internet. The suggestion that libraries will need to continue to strengthen their local collections, despite document delivery and electronic resources, is particularly valid, since the quantity of print material published each year is increasing rather than decreasing.

Prediction: "It is quite possible that demand [for document delivery] will be limited and that users will balk at paying the high fees that the suppliers will require to make the service profitable and viable".(1978)[6] In 1996, academic libraries were using document delivery services such as CARL UnCover, or were delivering books and photocopies to faculty offices at a much greater rate than was the case twenty years before. However, the volume of these transactions is still not high compared to the in-house and circulation use of the library. With the Internet and the Worldwide Web, it is possible that document delivery will change radically in character and that many more users will request delivery of information directly from suppliers rather than going through the library (another prognostication that has been a favorite of several writers in our field throughout the years). I suggest, though, that, for the next several years at least, document delivery, while increasing, will continue to be limited in comparison with the direct information delivery provided by libraries either through their traditional collections or with electronic resources that are available without charge to library users. Will users balk at paying fees? Probably not as much as they would have in the mid-1970s, before deregulation of various industries and change in the political temperament of the country (and indeed the world) made it more acceptable to charge for services and products that were once subsidized by the government. However, just as with library budgets, users' individual budgets are limited, and extensive document delivery, which requires a fee for each use probably, will not work.

Prediction: "Eventually the separate collections of the [RLG] member libraries will be viewed by users in the various libraries as a single massive distributed collection to which they can gain efficient access via on-line searching and the rapid delivery of requested items as well as by personal visits".(1979)[7] This statement was written in the very first year of the existence of RLG II, as the transformed Research Libraries Group came to be known. Two of the programs of RLG were resource-sharing and cooperative collection development; faculty from each member institution were also allowed access to the other institutions' libraries. The environment described by this prediction has not yet happened, but neither has it been completely superseded by changing events. It might still be possible for RLG's members to regard their collective holdings as a single large collection; that likelihood, however, will depend in large part on the extent to which the RLIN database is displayed and used as a single database, either by member institutions or elsewhere. The proliferation of other resources and the necessary dependence of libraries on multiple sources of information, suggest that another complementary prediction by De Gennaro might be a better indication of the future: "The National Library Network is the totality of the computer systems and on-line catalogs of the nation's libraries and networks."[8]

Prediction: "[Librarians] are still a long way...from developing...capabilities for dealing with recorded knowledge in the rapidly growing and changing variety of electronic formats such as magnetic tapes and magnetic, optical, and digital disks".(1983)[9] Obviously, since the time that this sentence was written, the explosion of the Internet has added the burden of dealing with yet another form of recorded knowledge to the already-full platter of the library. We still need to develop the capability for dealing with electronic information; services such as Yahoo and Lycos are good beginnings for the Internet/Web but are unlikely to solve the problem of defining the quality and relevance of information resources. That is a task that librarians are trained to accomplish and for which they will be praised if they are able to systematically, either singly or cooperatively, deal with the chaos that is the Internet today.

Prediction: "..Ideally, libraries would absorb the costs and provide free and unlimited access to their book, journal, and manuscript collections. The question of who pays for these new services is still unresolved, but I believe a consensus will emerge in favor of free access to locally held databases".(1986)[10] Librarians are still grappling with the question of how to pay for the increasing number of electronic resources, many of which are quite costly. Ideally, users would be fully subsidized by libraries for access to all of the information resources held locally; in reality, libraries must constantly evaluate the various complementary and competing products available as CD-ROM subscriptions, through the vendors of local on-line catalog systems, through utilities such as OCLC, or directly on tape from the publisher. Avoiding a pass-along charge for users may force a library to offer a less complete or sophisticated product. Will libraries be able to continue what has been a general practice of avoiding charges for locally held resources? Much depends upon the future financial health of the library, and librarians must make strong and effective arguments to funding sources for increased resources to support electronic as well as print collections.

Library of the future: information marketplace

In a seminal article entitled "Pay libraries and user charges," De Gennaro addressed the decreasing support for libraries, and suggested what the future might hold within an environment of constrained budgets, not dissimilar from the situation in which we now find ourselves.

Prediction: "It is possible that more libraries will offer free copying if and when the price is reduced to the point where the cost of monitoring the use of collecting the money begins to equal the fee. However, this is not likely."(1975)[11] At the risk of attempting to prove a negative hypothesis ('this is not likely'), we could view this statement as a prediction that has not yet been shown either correct or incorrect. With the proliferation of formats of materials, from local as well as remote locations, some libraries are discussing the provision of photocopies without charge, especially when the photocopies are a substitute for the purchase of a book, subscription, or database, and thus are similar to document delivery. As consumable items, however, photocopy workloads and costs are unpredictable and are difficult to build into a fixed budget without either jeopardizing other services or alienating users who might be asked to ration their copying. With equipment available to monitor printing from all kinds of devices and then allocate costs to the user, we are likely to witness more rather than less charging for photocopies.

Prediction: "If the library begins by offering...expensive services free like its traditional services, the demand will expand and eventually create an overload situation requiring some form of rationing based on rules or by the imposition of charges".(1975)[12] When libraries succeed beyond their wildest dreams, they run the risk of ultimate failure, because the expectations raised by the earlier success cannot be realized, and the original effort cannot be sustained. Closely related to the previous prediction, this prognostication is broader than the earlier reference to photocopying alone. Many libraries have experienced the flush of success with a new product or service, only to realize that without additional infusion of funds, staffing, or other support, an overwhelming response to a popular service must lead to 'failure,' even if this failure is defined only as the inability to keep up with the demand. The library at Georgetown University contains an Audio/Visual department which is responsible for classroom audio/visual and computing support. Going from 120 setups per month in the mid-1970s, to more than 8,000 setups per month in 1990, to more than 21,000 setups per month in 1995 requires an unlikely infusion of staff given the economic constraints typical of universities in the

'90s. The result is a rationing of this service, to the great dissatisfaction of the faculty who had become accustomed to calling up and receiving the service without problems.

Prediction: "Commercial, society, and university press publishers now rely to a very large and dangerous extent on library subscriptions to support their publications...This unhealthy system is going to end".(1977)[13] Almost twenty years later, the "unhealthy system" still has not gone by the board, although upheavals within the publishing industry and between librarians and publishers have become almost routine parts of our lives. Virtually every research and academic library in the United States has experienced one or more rounds of cancellation of periodical subscriptions since the late 1970s; at the same time, the Copyright Act of 1976 made publishers increasingly sensitive to the possibilities of 'new technological uses' of copyrighted works. Not coincidentally, the idea of saving money by sharing resources (and, presumably, purchasing fewer copies of any one title) became the center of scrutiny.

Publisher dependence on libraries continues to exist. Yes, libraries have canceled uncounted numbers of journal titles. In response, publishers raise the prices of the journals. Some libraries may feel compelled, because of faculty pressure or publisher monopoly of the field, to continue to subscribe to the journal, but a very large number of libraries continue to cancel titles whose increases of 50% or more for an annual subscription cost have finally become the straw that broke the back of the serials budget. Publishers of the very expensive, primarily scientific, journals have not experimented with a very simple marketing test: what would happen if the price of a journal *decreased* significantly? Perhaps nothing; but perhaps more libraries would subscribe -- because their budgets would finally allow them to, and, more to the point, perhaps individuals and other institutions would begin to subscribe, allowing the publishers to release their nearly total dependence on the library market. We hope that this "unhealthy system" will at last crumble in the face of more rational ways of doing business and making money.

Prediction: "The traditional spirit of cooperation among librarians will be sorely taxed as they start receiving an increasing number of computerized interlibrary loan requests from distant libraries with which they have no ties or affinity. The question of who pays...will become urgent and divisive..."(1979)[14] Solving the problem of who pays for interlibrary loan is already under way, with some of the solution coming almost by default, as some libraries charge in order to keep other libraries away -- a far cry from the cooperative spirit with which interlibrary lending began. In the late 1980s, the Research Libraries Group, which had traditionally offered free interlibrary loan within the membership, established a system whereby the net lenders would be reimbursed by the net borrowers. As long as interlibrary loan remains a relatively low-volume operation, there will be a small but persistent urgency on the part of those who are giving to ensure that they are rewarded in turn. State library systems have helped by reimbursing statewide net lenders with tax dollars, but as their ability to sustain this program diminishes, the issue of who pays and who gets may indeed divide our profession.

Prediction: "Free ILL in a multitype library network environment... will simply not be possible in the long run..."(1980)[15] This related prediction was couched within an explication for a foreign audience of the network structure in the United States, and the impact that rising rates of interlibrary loans were having on library budgets. Sixteen years later, we have reached an uncomfortable balance, with some free interlibrary loan, some cooperative (and, therefore, mostly free) interlibrary loan, some libraries charging for interlibrary loan, and a small number of libraries who do not lend their books at all. Similarly, charging for "non-returnables" (photocopies) is fairly commonplace, but the borrowing institution has the option of passing the charge along to the user or subsidizing the transaction. With highly constrained budgets in the 1990s, it is quite likely that an increasing number of libraries will find it necessary to charge for this service that, after all, takes their collections away from the users for whom they were originally purchased. Despite the good intentions of cooperation, a perceived lack of mutual benefit will drive libraries to retreat from offering these services free to other institutions.

Prediction: "Pay libraries [will not displace] free libraries or... free libraries [inhibit] the development of for-profit information services".(1982)[16] This prediction was a response to the nascent Information Industry Association's claim that pay libraries were inevitable. De Gennaro suggested that while pay information services might have their own place in the information infrastructure, there would always be an essential "free library" component within our society. One might comment that the issues at hand in this argument are no longer valid and that the prediction has been superseded by intervening events. This writer would disagree. As library budgets become more constrained, there is increasing pressure on librarians, by their boards or their administrations, to make money and to pay for themselves, to the furthest extent possible. Charging for services would, of course, bring libraries into competition with the many commercial information services that have arisen in the past two decades. But, more importantly, libraries have a clientele to serve; offering their services for pay would deflect their attention from their primary clientele, and would impoverish the very community that is relying on that library for information services. Moreover, librarians are not trained to be business people; most entered the field because they wanted to provide services, not charge for them.

Library of the future: management and administration

In another critically important article, "Shifting gears: information technology and the academic library," De Gennaro made a number of predictions, many of which were borne out in the years that followed. But a few predictions have not yet been fulfilled; the topics that they address are slower-moving than the very rapid-paced technologically or entrepreneurially oriented issues discussed in so many of his articles.

Prediction: "As the information world grows, the relative influence of traditional libraries diminishes".(1979)[17] This statement of fact is treated as a prediction for the purposes of this paper. The relative influence of *traditional* libraries has clearly diminished. Less than 25 years ago, libraries were the "only game in town" for matters relating to research materials; there was no organized information industry, and publishers just published. Now there is much competition for the role once held exclusively by libraries; in that sense, there has certainly been a diminution of influence. However, with the critical need to make sense out of the maelstrom that the Information Age has become, even the ordinary citizen recognizes that the skills and knowledge of the librarian will be vitally important to sort the wheat from the chaff, and the valid from the invalid, and to present the information in some meaningful way to the ultimate users of the information. It is proposed that in the coming years, if librarians take on the role that is being offered them, the influence of the library profession will be regained.

Prediction: "Library and information services will cost more in the future than they do now, but they will be far more effective".(1983)[18] The first part of this sentence is not at issue. Libraries <u>do</u> cost more than they did a decade ago, and we assume that they will cost even more in the future. Even when indexing for constant dollars, the cost of libraries has increased if for no other reason than the necessity for adding technologies rather than replacing them. The critical point here, though, is whether and when libraries will be more effective than they were in the past. This writer's view is that by whatever means necessary, librarians must ensure that libraries will be more effective and perceived to be indispensable to their users in the future. We have not reached that point yet, but the visionaries in the field are urging the entire profession to step forward and reach for the ring that is being offered -- as the rest of the world agrees that it is the skills and training of librarians that makes them ideally suited to bring order to the chaos that is the Internet and to provide guidance to information resources in the future. The medical and school librarians have adopted structures which encourage and enable them to focus upon the quality of their work; it is time for the remainder of the library profession to make their libraries more effective by becoming more effective themselves as professionals, in four specific areas: service to library users should be creative and expanded from its current level-- it needs to go beyond the walls of the library building to reach the user wherever he or she is with whatever information can address that user's needs; library professionals must create strategic partnerships with related professions such as publishing or telecommunications; risk-taking and creativity must be present to be an organization that is unusual, stellar, and meets the needs of the information-seeking public of the late 20th century; and increased focus on recruitment and retention is needed to identify and attract excellent young people into the profession, whether from college or secondary school.

Prediction: "In many cases, it will not be feasible to acquire the data [in house], and we will have to provide access to it on demand".(1983)[19] The management of information, particularly the way in which libraries must balance the strengthening of traditional collections with the adoption of new formats, continues to be a problem for many libraries. The prediction articulated here presaged the "just in time/just in case" philosophies that are under so much discussion recently. Now, as then, there is not a clear-cut answer to the question of how to provide all the information needed and wanted by one's users within the budget made available. Within a research library -- or even a four-year college library -- is "just in time" an adequate principle for the provision of information to students and faculty? Or is it better to be safe and ensure that as much of the information that one's community of users might need is held by the library, ready for the moment that they decide they wish to use it? We propose that a wise manager of library collections will be able to carefully identify that corpus of information that should be owned by the library if it is to succeed at its mission and, therefore, be able to articulate a philosophy for those materials that will be acquired on a "just in time" basis. But we are not there yet; there is a misunderstanding of the principles involved in "just in time," as well as strong ties to the traditional ways of doing things -- "just in case." Time, indeed, will tell if we will successfully identify information to be acquired on demand.

Prediction: "The rate of growth of collections will continue to decline in the next decade as it has in the last, and emphasis on electronic access will grow. As the cost of constructing and maintaining new stack spaces continues to rise, libraries will turn increasingly to off-site storage and to the use of mobile compact shelving where floor capacities exist".(1983)[20] Libraries have not seen the end of space issues. From a "bottomless pit" in the 1960s and 1970s, to a highly technological organization which, nonetheless, must continue to collect traditional materials, libraries and their parent organizations cannot seem to come to terms with whether or not collections will grow and whether or not new space is appropriate. The decrease in collecting during the late 1970s turned out to be a temporary faltering in the inexorable growth of research and academic library collections. Even the budgetary setbacks of the 1990s, serious as they have been, have not prevented libraries from continuing to build their collections and provide access to electronic resources. The surprising phenomenon has been the rather large number of new library buildings or new additions to existing libraries that have been built, and continue to be built. Simultaneously, compact shelving is being installed, and remote storage facilities supplement the central library buildings. It is as though we want our cake and eat it too, and are being able, for the most part, to do so. This trend may not be able to continue, but there is no bottoming out apparent on the horizon.

Prediction: "Financial resources will be found to fund library transitions [and retooling] in an increasing number of universities".(1983)[21] In retrospect, it is remarkable how many libraries have been given the resources to purchase integrated library systems, build information arcades and labs, and otherwise change the nature of the organization into one that is vastly different from its predecessor. However, with technology requiring replacement at least every three years now, if not more frequently, the ability of libraries and their parent organizations to keep up with upgrades, replacement parts, and enhancements will be sorely tested. The corporate and foundation programs that generously supported the introduction of information technologies into libraries in the 1980s have turned their attention to other problems and cannot be relied upon as a means of support; nor, as we have observed earlier, can the government programs that used to be available to cultural institutions such as libraries. So, we hope that De Gennaro's projection is correct; only time will tell.

Prediction: "In the on-line environment the need to maintain...rigid space arrangements will disappear and we will have the freedom and flexibility to rearrange and revise our spaces and services".(1987)[22] As far back as twenty-five years ago, librarians began to experiment with new ways of organizing libraries, sometimes to take advantage of apparent flexibility offered by innovative information technologies and sometimes to adopt new management technique or fads. Often, libraries experimenting with extreme forms of rearrangement found that the older and more traditional models had a rational basis in management principle, and they returned to those models or a version thereof. Nevertheless, we are now able to think about renovations and rearrangements without, for example, creating the bubble diagram that shows how many departments and user services need to be close to the card catalog. Distribution of information on workstations scattered throughout library facilities has already created a natural evolution in the way librarians work -- even when there has not been a formal administrative restructuring. When libraries perform a strategic planning exercise to articulate goals and objectives for the future, they will take advantage of windows of opportunity to realign departments, services, and space. But the organizational model, which basically divides the library into public services and technical services departments, seems to persist, resisting efforts to design a totally new way of doing business.

Library of the future: networking and automation

Many of De Gennaro's writings on networking and automation are among his earliest and tend to be more descriptive and analytical rather than predictive. A sizable number of the predictions made in his technology-oriented papers having already been proven correct and need not be discussed here but a selection are included in Appendix A. Below are a few prognostications that remain elusive.

Prediction: "To make it politically and practically feasible for academic research libraries to abandon finally the traditional models and the chimeric goal of self-sufficiency while at the same time improving their ability to fulfill their research functions, an effective national library network will have to be created".(1975)[23] In those days, the development of the Library of Congress, OCLC, and the regional networks appeared to be heading directly for a large and formally established national network. Had such a network come into being, the presumption was that it would assist all kinds of libraries to serve their users more effectively. What happened, of course, was that the influence of the Library of Congress diminished significantly, and the putative national network never materialized as a formal structure. In its place, we have an informal national network, plus the tools made available through the Internet, the Worldwide Web, and similar developing structures. These structures and tools will, in all likelihood, perform the same kind of task as the earlier national library network would have done -- to allow libraries to justify abandoning traditional models and place reliance on information located at other locations.

Prediction: "The implementation of [computer-based networks] in nearly 2000 libraries during a single decade has made change in libraries a way of life. Its effects will multiply and accelerate and will lead to a sweeping transformation of libraries in the next decade".(1979)[24] Libraries in the 1990s do not look very much like the libraries of the 1970s, but the sweeping transformation referred to in this quotation has not yet taken place. A transformation of this nature will be completed by the end of the first decade of the 21st century, when libraries have fully engaged the most sophisticated features of the information revolution. At the same time, institutional budgets and their constraints will have forced librarians to face with realism and determination the question of how to continue to serve as a critical link in the knowledge transmission process.

Prediction: "Traditional cataloging may go the way of hand bookbinding...With production at a few books a day per cataloger, traditional original cataloging, like hand binding, has also priced itself out of the market".(1981)[25] When AACR2 was implemented, original cataloging slowed to a snail's pace, making the copy cataloging being done by using automated systems and networks look like a manager's dream in comparison. Traditional cataloging has not gone the way of the dinosaur, although there are certainly fewer catalogers than there once were.

Now librarians are discussing how to catalog the Internet or the Web and how to incorporate into local on-line catalogs the information about resources not held locally but made available either through interlibrary loan, document delivery, or on-line. Perhaps we will see "traditional cataloging" diminish in quantity, to be replaced by the organization of knowledge in these new formats. As long as there are resources to catalog (including books) and as long as our "national library" -- the Library of Congress -- has sufficient budgetary constraints that it can no longer act as the master cataloger for all the libraries of the nation, there will be catalogers!

Prediction: "On-line systems are providing powerful new subject and word search capabilities which will increase access to collections and begin to make many of our traditional subject cataloging and classification conventions redundant or obsolete".(1981)[26] The dream of the 1980's was that full texts would be analyzed using the indexes and tables of contents of books. While that dream did not come to pass, this prediction can be equally applied to the search tools and browsers for the Worldwide Web, such as the aforementioned Lycos and Yahoo. We are now discovering that even these relatively sophisticated mechanisms are inadequate to truly gain control of the information available on the Web, and there is still opportunity for librarians to step forward and use available technologies and their knowledge of the organization of information to increase reasonable access to the world of information now at our disposal -- if only we could reach it!

Prediction: "Our society will have to get accustomed to paying much higher prices for [information] in the future, as it has with energy in the last decade".(1981)[27] The difference was that society was at least used to paying *something* for energy. People are or have been used to getting information free. The directions being taken by the government and by libraries that can no longer subsidize access to multiple information resources all point toward a requirement that library users or the institutions that provide their library service pay much higher prices in the future than they have in the past. Decisions on whether and how to subsidize the end user are made on a local basis, of course, and the impact on users can be softened tremendously by a library and institutional administration willing and able to identify what resources ought to be provided at no cost and what should require a payment. The potential change in the Copyright Act could serve notice to librarians and to the citizens of this country that information can no longer be perceived as a free good. The Jeffersonian contention that government and other information are essential for the educated electorate required in a democracy may well have gone by the board.

Conclusion

It is evident that the thoughtful analyses provided by De Gennaro over the years for the library and information profession have had a significant impact. The prognostications that he correctly made (see Appendix A) suggest that the remaining ones, discussed in this paper, have an excellent chance of also proving to be correct. As such, they can continue to provide guidance to library administrators and others working to achieve the best possible environment for libraries and their users in the years to come, despite fairly significant odds.

De Gennaro's writing spans an active and important part of the library profession's existence. To reread his works is to relive vividly some exciting times -- and to come across statements that are amusing or revealing in today's context. Among these are: "OCLC interlibrary loan requests appear to be leveling off at the rate of about 3,500 per day."[28] Or from the same paper, in a discussion of on-line search services, is the comment that it is too soon to know whether on-line searching can become a profitable business. Two particularly prescient passages suggest the coming of on-line systems and of OCLC, at a time when neither existed:

> "When it becomes economically feasible to store such a large data file in a direct access device and to search and manipulate it from a cathode ray tube console, the possibilities for making interesting and novel uses of the data will be expanded enormously...it will probably be several years before it will be economically feasible in a research library environment. It seems idle, therefore, to speculate about these interesting but relatively remote possibilities"[29] ;

and finally

> "instead of actually producing a computer printout of a segment of the LC shelflist to be used for comparison [with other libraries' cataloging], it could be in random access storage and accessible through a cathode-ray tube or visual display console. The local card shelflist entries would be searched in sequence by calling for the appropriate part of the alphabet on the console display unit. Each time a match was encountered a symbol would be added to the machine record together with the local call number and any other necessary local information."[30]

OCLC, anyone?

Let us hope that the library profession will continue to appreciate and benefit from the powerful and, in many cases, truly accurate predictions by De Gennaro -- a scholar of futurism for our field.

Appendix

Selected prognostications judged to have been proven correct

The citations for these statements are all from Richard De Gennaro's *Libraries, Technology, and the Information Marketplace: Selected Papers*. (Boston, MA: GK. Hall & Co., 1987).

"Technology and Access," 1986
1. "The new optical disk technology will not superseded the existing archives of microforms, but it will probably supersede the medium for making and distributing new comprehensive collections of research materials," p.10.
2. "The new technology will not make existing collections of books and journals obsolete and unnecessary, but the collections will no longer be the only or even the primary resources of the library of the future," p.10.

3. "...technology is, in fact, putting libraries into business," p.17.

"Online Catalogs and Integrated Systems," 1986
1. "...soon [users] will be asking for access to the full text online, and not just the catalog records," p.22.
2. "Indeed, there will soon be no place in the market for vendors of stand-alone components such as the online catalog, circulation, or serials control," p.22.

"Electronic Data Files: the New Frontier," 1986
1. "The library's task in the coming years is to develop appropriate policies, strategies, and technologies for providing access to published as well as unpublished electronic files...," p.32.
2. "...a consensus will emerge in favor of free access to locally held databases," p.33.

"Libraries and Computer Centers in the Wired University," 1986.
1. "[Some of the newcomers in the information game in university] will persevere and succeed in carving out important roles for themselves...those who succeed will not put the library out of business any more than the successful commercial information providers did," p.39.
2. "I do not think we are going to see many true mergers of libraries and computer centers in the next ten years," p.40.

"Libraries, Technology, and the Information Marketplace," 1981.
1. "[Lancaster's prediction of a paper less society by the year 2000 will be proven to be mere speculation or science fiction,]" p.49.
2. "Libraries cannot exist without librarians and librarians cannot exist without libraries. The names may change in the future, but their functions will continue as long as there are users who need to gain access to the record in whatever form it takes...," p.54.
3. "[Commercial full-text providers] will create and satisfy a whole new market for those services, and libraries will be part of that market," p.60.

"Research Libraries Enter the Information Age," 1979.
1. "...the solutions to our research library problems are not to be found primarily in Washington, but in the voluntary and concerted actions of a peer group of research libraries with a common need and a common interest in solving those problems," p.79.
2. "online bibliographic searching [will] combine with online ordering and eventually with online document delivery of the documents cited," p.81.

"Copyright, Resource Sharing, and Hard Times," 1977
1. "Resource sharing will not seriously erode publishers' profits, nor will it help libraries as much as they think," p.99.

"Escalating Journal Prices: Time to Fight Back," 1977
2. "As long as librarians continue to buy at ever-increasing prices without protest, the publishers will continue to raise prices and multiply titles," p.110.

"Providing Bibliographic Services from Machine-Readable Data Bases: the Library's Role," 1973
1. "Librarians will play a key role in facilitating access to data bases by functioning as the interface or broker between the user on campus and [the] regional and special processing and distribution centers," p. 135.

"Shifting Gears: Information Technology and the Academic Library," 1983
1. "Library and information services will cost more in the future than they do now, but they will be far more effective," p.144.

"Matching Commitments to Needs and Resources," 1983
1. "[...there will be] a serious long-term reduction in our ability to maintain the kind of research collections, services, and facilities that scholars have traditionally demanded and that librarians have tried to provide," p.168.

"Impact of On-line Services on the Academic Library," 1977
1. "On-line services could become one of the important driving forces in a larger context of change," p.202.
2. "Rising prices, declining budgets, and increased resource sharing will help bring about the demise of many journals," p.202.

"Austerity, Technology, and Resource Sharing: Research Libraries Face the Future," 1975
1. "The traditional emphasis on developing large local research collections must be shifted toward developing excellent local working collections and truly effective means of gaining access to needed research material," p.211.

"Library Automation and Networking: Perspectives on Three Decades," 1983
1. "...library administrators will move to regain much of the control over their own operations and decision-making that they gave up to the networks in the 1970's," p.255.

"Doing Business With Vendors in the Computer-based Library Systems Marketplace," 1978
1. "...the systems will get better and cheaper with the passage of time," p.304.

"Development and Administration of Automated Systems in Academic Libraries," 1968
1. "The justification of computer-based library systems on the basis of costs alone will continue to be difficult because machine systems not only replace manual systems but generally do more and different things, and it is extremely difficult to compare them with the old manual systems, which frequently did not adequately do the job they were supposed to do and for which operating costs often were unknown," p.385.

Notes

1. De Gennaro, Richard. *Libraries, Technology, and the Information Marketplace: Selected Papers*. Boston: G.K. Hall & Co., 1987. p.46.

2. Ibid., p.48.

3. Toffler, Alvin. *Future Shock*. New York, Random House: 1970.

4. De Gennaro, p.237.

5. --- Library Automation: Changing Patterns and New Directions. *Library Journal*, (January 1, 1976): 175-83.

6. --- Copyright, Resource Sharing, and Hard Times: A View from the Field. *American Libraries* September 1977.

7. --- Research Libraries Enter the Information Age. *Library Journal* November 15, 1979.

8. --- Library Automation and Networking: Perspectives on Three Decades. *Library Journal*, (April 1, 1983): 629-35.

9. --- op.cit., p.32.

10. --- op.cit., p.33.

11. --- Pay Libraries and User Charges. *Library Journal*, (February 15,1975): 263-67.

12. Ibid.

13. --- Escalating Journal Prices: Time to Fight Back. *American Libraries*, February 1977.

14. --- Research Libraries Enter the Information Age. *Library Journal*, November 15, 1979.

15. --- Computer Network Systems: The Impact of Technology on Co-Operative Interlending in the U.S.A. *Interlending Review* 9, no: 2 (1981).

16. --- Libraries, Technology, and the Information Marketplace. *Library Journal*, June 1, 1982.

17. --- Research Libraries Enter the Information Age." *Library Journal*, November 15, 1979.

18. --- "Shifting Gears: Information Technology and the Academic Library. *Library Journal*, June 15, 1984.

19. Ibid.

20. Ibid.

21. Ibid.

22. --- *Libraries, technology, and the information marketplace: selected papers.* Boston. K. Hall & Co., 1987. p.26.

23. --- Austerity, Technology, and Resource Sharing: Research Libraries Face the Future. *Library Journal,* (May 15, 1975): 917-923.

24. --- The Role of the Academic Library in Networking. *Networks for Networkers.* Edited by Barbara E. Markuson and Blanche Woolls. New York: Neal Schuman, 1980. p.304-08.

25. --- Libraries and Networks in Transition: Problems and Prospects for the 1980's. *Library Journal,* (March 15, 1981): 1045-49.

26. Ibid.

27. Ibid.

28. --- Computer Network Systems: The Impact of Technology on Co-Operative Interlending in the U.S.A."

29. --- Harvard University's Widener Library Shelflist Conversion and Publication Program *College and Research Libraries,* September 1970.

30. --- "A Strategy for the Conversion of Research Library Catalogs to Machine Readable Form. *College and Research Libraries* (July 1967): 253-57.

Digital Libraries are Much More than Digitized Collections and Services.

by Paul Evan Peters

> The information superhighway is about the global movement of weightless
> bits at the speed of light... [It] may be mostly hype today, but it is an
> understatement about tomorrow.[1]

Introduction

The term "digital library" has recently come into use to refer to the realization of our most ambitious dreams for the application of high-performance computers and networks to the production, management, and utilization of knowledge in research, educational, and other communities. It synthesizes the "bits on silicon rather than ink on paper" core concept of the term "electronic library" with the "not only what you own but what you have access to" one of "virtual library." It has generally replaced both of these two prior terms of art.

But there is more going on in the emergence of this term than the quest for more efficient language. A shift of mind-set away from building systems for networking printed and other analog information toward building systems for managing networked information is also gathering momentum. Although most contemporary digital libraries are being built to manage digitized versions of things that were already available in analog formats (e.g. books, periodicals, and video and sound recordings), a steadily increasing number are now being built to manage "digital" rather than "digitized" information.

The "knowledge objects" enabled by this emergent class of digital libraries will be much more like "experiences" than they will be like "things," much more like "programs" than "documents," and readers will have unique experiences with these objects in even more profound ways than is already the case with books, periodicals, etc. The relativity principle that from Einstein forward we have taken for granted as applying to physical space, and which modern western philosophers since Immanuel Kant have worried might also apply to our *knowledge* of physical space, has become one of the central, if not the central, information system design challenges in cyberspace.

This paper will explore the concept of "relativistic" or "non-Newtonian" information systems, and will develop the view that they are systems that support the production, management, and utilization of "low mass, high velocity" rather than "high mass, low velocity" (such as ink on paper) knowledge. The role of libraries and librarians with respect to these systems will also be discussed.

Proposition

We need a new theory of knowledge, a new epistemology for networked information environments. We may even need more than one. This new theory should explain, among other things, why knowledge objects are the way they are and why knowledge agents do the things they do in networked environments. We need to frame and then address questions like "What is knowledge?" and "What is knowing?" for users of the "low mass, high velocity" information systems that are enabled by high performance, wide-area, digital networks. We should expect quite different results from those produced by theories for "high mass, low velocity" information systems. We should expect results that are very much more situational and social. We should expect a "non-Newtonian" theory of knowledge in which the emphasis is very much more on knowledge creators and users than it is on knowledge objects.

Discussion

Fortunately, the search for this new, non-Newtonian theory of knowledge has already begun.

> Since Newton had shown "nature" to be a closed and complete system, words should be too. Ideally, in a Newtonian society, you wouldn't need words at all, sincere ideals and clear feelings of physical entities would do it all. You look through words to the goods that are really out there in the real world. ... All this changes in an information society. There, the words <u>are</u> the "goods." They operate in an ambiguous fashion, overlapping, bumping into one another, creating unintended meanings, making more meaning come out of an utterance that the author put into it. ... The immateriality of information brings with it a new set of boundary conditions [2]

> Knowledge in this new system shares much of the mathematical relativity from which it was born. Its certainties are interim versions of an unending text, the totality of which the computer can give us access to. In passing from analogue signal to digital we seem to be also passing from the objective view of knowledge - which has been in decline throughout the century for other reasons - to the relativistic, endlessly interpretative view of knowledge. It is a final working through into our culture of the relatively doctrine with which the century began. [3]

Still, the task ahead is enormous. We must now rethink our approach to information systems in virtually the same ways that 20th Century physicists have completely rethought their approaches to physical systems. These scientists discovered that matter at high velocities, on the one hand, and with low masses, on the other, behaves quite differently than does the "low velocity, high mass" matter that occupied Newton's attention. First, they developed "special" theories. Lately they have been developing general, unified "theories of everything," as they've come to put it. Physicists have been at this task for most of the 20th Century. Now it is our turn to join them in pondering how God plays dice.

"Frames of reference" and other "observer variables" will be central to the new, non-Newtonian theory of knowledge, just as they are to non-Newtonian theories of matter. Such effects are already obvious in existing information systems. Each of us clearly takes a different meaning away from the same book, and we draw different lessons from the same experience. What's more, "knowledge" is commonly understood to be "trustworthy information," and most of us rely overwhelmingly upon the experience of others rather than our own, direct, personal experience for assessing "trustworthiness." Most existing theories of knowledge do not address these realities at all. They prefer instead to attribute the indeterminacy of knowledge to human imperfection. We can afford no such hand-waving in our new theory of knowledge.

The situational and social character of knowledge has long been a concern of sociologists of knowledge, particularly so to theorists of the "social construction of reality."

> All interpretation of this world is based upon a stock of previous experiences of it, our own experiences and those handed down to us by our parents and teachers, which is in the form of "knowledge at hand," function as a scheme of reference. ... [T]he world is from the outset not the private world of the single individual but an intersubjective world common to all of us, in which we have not a theoretical but an eminently practical interest.[4]

> In the beginning of this paper we referred to William James' theory of the many sub-universes each of which may be conceived as reality after its own fashion. ... In order to free this important insight from its psychologistic setting we prefer to speak instead of ... finite provinces of meaning upon each of which we may bestow the accent of reality. We speak of provinces of meaning and not of sub-universes because it is the meaning of our experiences and not the ontological structure of the objects which constitutes reality. Hence we call a certain set of our experiences a finite province of meaning if all of them show a specific cognitive style and are - with respective to this style - not only consistent in themselves but also compatible with one another.[5]

Non-Euclidean theories of geometry, drawn from mathematics and not physics, provided 20th Century physicists with the means to predict, explain, and even control the behavior of "high velocity, low mass" matter in physical systems. Perhaps theories of the social construction of reality, drawn from sociology and not philosophy, will provide us with what we need to do likewise with respect to "high velocity, low mass" knowledge in information systems.

This work will most likely be completed by those who are growing up taking the Internet and personal computers for granted as much as we took broadcasting and radio and television sets for granted.

> "[Real Life] is just one more window," [Doug, a midwestern college junior] repeats, "and it's not usually my best one." ... What is real? That question

may take many forms. What are we willing to count as real? What do our models allow us to see as real? To what degree are we willing to take simulations for reality? How do we keep a sense that there is reality distinct from simulation? Would that sense itself be an illusion? ... Today's children are growing up in the computer culture; all the rest of us are at best its naturalized citizens.[6]

Until then, we should redouble out efforts to unlearn the theories of knowledge we received from our predecessors and to develop a new theory that is more adequate to the networked information environment and to the tasks we want to accomplish there.

Unlike information processing [artificial intelligence research and development], which looked to programs and specific locations for information storage, the connectionists did not see information as being stored anywhere in particular. Rather it was inherent everywhere. The system's information, like information in the brain, would be evoked rather than found.[7]

Application

Non-Newtonian information systems (i.e., information systems that enable us to create, manage, and use "high velocity, low mass" knowledge) will intensely focus on and be extensively determined by the needs, skills, and preferences of individual knowledge creators and users. The networked information environment permits (even demands) that broadcasting to large, relatively undifferentiated audiences give way to "narrowcasting" to considerably smaller, differentiated audiences. But, even more important, it permits interactive "pointcasting" among members of highly dynamic communities of interest. The "mass customization" of resources and services in the networked information environment implies that "knowledge" does not exist apart from the interaction of information system users with themselves and with the system's resources and services.

In non-Newtonian information systems knowledge creators and users will command greater attention from information professionals and enterprises, including librarians and libraries, than will knowledge objects. The networked information environment allows creators and users to assume direct responsibility for many of the information production and utilization activities that information professionals and enterprises have been doing for them. Soon, these creators and users will also be able to assume direct responsibility for managing the information that is most important to them. In essence, each knowledge creator and user will have, to one degree or another, her or his own highly individualized model of the networked information environment, a model that is realized in the hardware and software platform by which he or she operates in that environment.

Information professionals and enterprises will bear the prime responsibility for providing the technological, intellectual, social, historical, financial, and other contexts which allow shared communities of interest to emerge, sometimes in unexpected and surprising ways, from these highly individualized models. As Rayport and Sviokla have explored in two recent articles[8], "context" is one of the three most important variables for generating recognizable, rewardable value in the networked information environment.

- Platforms: The mechanisms by which products and services are actually delivered.
- Content: The ways in which a given product or service differs in substance from alternative products and services.
- Context: The settings in which access to a given product or service is allowed, usually together with other complementary, and even competing, products and services.

In general, non-Newtonian information systems deal with each of these in a much more flexible fashion than do Newtonian ones. Many Newtonian systems ignore, often tacitly, the context variable altogether. They present themselves as the one and only context in which certain information is available, focusing on prohibiting or controlling rather than enabling or informing access and use. Decoupling content from context so that knowledge creators and users can assume direct responsibility for the former and information professionals and enterprises can focus on the latter is an immediate challenge of practical as well as theoretical importance.

In a new environment, such as the gravity field of the moon, laws of physics play out differently. On the Net, there is an equivalent change in "gravity" brought about by the ease of information transfer. We are entering a new economic environment - as different as the moon is from the earth - where a new set of physical rules will govern what intellectual property means, how opportunities are created from it, who prospers, and who loses.[9]

Chief among the new rules is that "content is free." While not all content will be free, the new economic dynamic will operate as if it were. In the world of the Net, content (including software) will serve as advertising for services such as support, aggregation, filtering, assembly, and integration of content modules, or training of customers in their use. ... I am not saying that content is worthless, or that you will always get it for free. Content providers should manage their businesses *as if* it were free, and then figure out how to set up relationships or develop ancillary products and services that cover the costs of developing content. Or players may simply try their hands at creative endeavors based on service, not content assets: filtering content, hosting on-line forums, rating others' (free) content, custom programming, consulting, or performing. The creator who writes off the costs of developing content immediately - as if it were valueless - is always going to win over the creator who can't figure out how to cover those costs. The way to become a leading content provider may be to start by giving your content away. This "generosity" isn't a moral decision: it's a business strategy.[10]

Intellectual value (some call it context) is also simply the presence of other
people, often specific ones, interacting casually or formally. ... The
intellectual value of context can't be replicated so easily over the Net.
Unsurprisingly, it depends on the activity or presence of a person - locally or
remotely, in real time or at least in individual response. Intellectual property
is the embodiment or automation of effort, replicable easily for all.
Intellectual value, on the other hand, is the effort, service, or process itself:
it can sometimes be shared, but the effort can't be replicated without another
person around to do the same task.[11]

Conclusion

This paper has explored the concept of "relativistic" or "non-Newtonian" information
systems, and has developed the view that they are systems that support the production,
management, and utilization of "low mass, high velocity" rather than "high mass, low velocity"
knowledge. It has also suggested a key role for information professionals and enterprises, such as
librarians and libraries, to play in the networked information environment, a role that is important,
to say the least, and quite different, in degree if not in type, from the role that they are playing now.
This paper sought to map, however tentatively, a new direction for thinking about "digital
libraries," one that is completely different from the direction taken when thinking about "digitized
collections and services." Information professionals and enterprises need a paradigm shift rather
than a paradigm drift if we are to serve the individuals and communities we must serve in the 21st
Century. This paper has endeavored to contribute momentum toward this much needed shift.

Acknowledgments

Although I first encountered the "high mass, low velocity" versus "low mass, high velocity"
distinction in Nicholas Negroponte's *Being Digital* [12], I cannot say I gave it much thought until I
heard it used in an off-the-cuff comment by Daniel E. Atkins, Dean, School of Information and
Library Studies, University of Michigan, at a symposium on the transformation of public libraries
in December, 1995. I also wish to acknowledge the effect of C. West Churchman [13] and Burkhart
Holzner [14] [15] on my thinking about the importance of frames of reference, observer variables, and
the sociology of knowledge in general; I am sure that both of these authors will figure prominently
in my future writings about non-Newtonian information systems. Finally, I wish to acknowledge
my debt to Richard De Gennaro, in whose honor the papers in this volume have been prepared. I
cannot resist closing with a characterization of the sort of Newtonian thinking that Dick has pushed
against his entire career, and which he has dedicated his life to helping those of us who have had
the pleasure to work with him to overcome.

It is interesting to note just how Newtonian most organizations are. The
machine imagery of the spheres was captured by organizations in an
emphasis on structure and parts. Responsibilities have been organized into
functions. People have been organized into roles. Page after page of
organizational charts depict the workings of the machine: the number of
pieces, what fits where, who the big pieces are. ... This reduction into parts

and the proliferation of separations has characterized not just organizations, but everything in the world in the past three hundred years. Knowledge was broken into disciplines and subjects, engineering became a prized discipline, and people were fragmented - counseled to use different parts of themselves in different settings.[16]

Notes

1. Negroponte, p 12.

2. Lanham, p. 229.

3. Smith, p. 2.

4. Schutz, 1971, p. 208.

5. Ibid pp. 229-230.

6. Turkle, pp. 13, 73, 78.

7. Ibid p. 132.

8. Rayport and Sviokla, p. 75.

9. Dyson, p. 137.

10. Ibid pp. 137-138.

11. Ibid p. 138.

12. Negroponte, p. 12.

13. Churchman.

14. Holzner.

15. Holzner and Marx.

16. Wheatley, p. 27.

Bibliography

Churchman, C. West. *The Design of Inquiring Systems: Basic Concepts of Systems and Organization.* New York: Basic Books, 1971.

Dyson, Esther. "Intellectual Value," *Wired* 3:7 (July 1995) 136.

Holzner, Burkart and John Marx. *Knowledge Application: The Knowledge System in Society.* Boston: Allyn and Bacon, 1979.

Holzner, Burkart. *Reality Construction in Society*. Cambridge, MA: Schenkman Pub. Co, 1968.
Lanham, Richard A. *The Electronic Word: Democracy, Technology, and the Arts*. Chicago: The University of Chicago Press, 1993.

Negroponte, Nicholas. *Being Digital*. New York: Alfred A. Knopf, 1995.
Rayport, J. F. and J. J.Sviokla. "Exploiting the Virtual Value Chain." *Harvard Business Review* 73:6 (November/December 1995): 75.

Schutz, Alfred. *Reflections on the Problem of Relevance*. New Haven: Yale University Press, 1970.

Schutz, Alfred. *Collected Papers I: The Problem of Social Reality*. The Hague: Martinus Nijhoff, 1971.

Smith, Anthony. *Books to Bytes: The Computer and the Library*. New York: Columbia University, Gannett Center for Media Studies, Occasional Paper No. 7. November 1988.

Turkle, Sherry. *Life on the Screen: Identity in the Age of the Internet.* New York, NY: Simon & Schuster, 1995.

Wheatley, Margaret J. *Leadership and the New Science: Learning about Organization from an Orderly Universe*. San Francisco: Berrett-Kohler Publishers, 1992.

Addressing the Challenges Facing Research Libraries:
A Generation of Leaders with Impact

by Duane E. Webster

Introduction and summary

Over the past two decades, a generation of library leaders has successfully engaged the challenges facing the continued development of research libraries. At the outset of this period, research library missions centered around a library's capacity to provide access to information by acquiring a significant percentage of world-wide information resources. This traditional mission involved the acquisition, management, and servicing of large collections of print materials primarily for use by local scholars and students. During the last two decades however, research libraries began to move toward a transformed concept of the research library mission. A recent landmark report on scholarly communication and research libraries by The Andrew W. Mellon Foundation confirmed what many library leaders knew only too well: that economic pressures and publishing practices undermined the ability of even the largest research institutions to sustain these comprehensive, print-based collections.[1]

Leaders in the research library community understand this dilemma and are enthusiastically engaging these pressures as they prepare for the future. The research library of tomorrow will be able to connect the curious user with information in any format, at any time, and at a cost that society can sustain. This new future involves establishing "virtual" libraries of electronically accessible research collections that are viewed and serviced as a collection of shared, networked resources for the advancement of scholarship, learning, and society as a whole.

One illustration of this transformation in mission is the change in the requirements for membership in the Association of Research Libraries. At the start of the seventies, membership in ARL was determined solely by qualitative measures that described the character and nature of investments made by the university in the library (e.g. expenditures, size of collection, level of acquisitions). The intent was to measure objectively the similarity of the prospective institution with the historical membership of the association.

Today, the requirements for ARL membership have been expanded to examine qualitative criteria aimed at understanding the potential contribution of the library to the collections and services of the aggregate of research libraries in North America. While a prospective member must still look and perform like a research library (in quantitative terms), there is a new recognition that the library must also demonstrate that it can make a distinctive contribution to the emerging distributed research collections.

The leadership assignment for the 90's is navigating this transition: from a traditional, well understood mission supported by an extraordinary partnership between scholars and librarians, to a new future populated with different players that strains relationships among traditional partners. Of primary importance is that the transformation be consciously shaped so that it is in the interest of the research and higher education community - not inadvertently evolved from forces external to our environment.

Research library leaders are acting aggressively to find ways to influence scholarly communication in a cost effective manner and manage and provide access to information in the electronic information age. Already, much is being done at local, regional, and national levels to promote innovation in library services to students, faculty, researchers, and scholars. There is a great deal of focus on and excitement in moving toward new directions for research libraries. The following review highlights several of the more important accomplishments achieved by a generation of research library leaders during a period of tumultuous change and illustrates the array of challenges that need to be engaged by those who lead libraries into the 21st century.

Collections

Dramatic increases in the cost, volume, and formats of scholarly information have fundamentally altered the processes for collecting and disseminating information in support of North American education and research. A marked characteristic of the past two decades is the explosive growth of print information materials. Internationally, 1,000 books are published each day and the total of all printed output doubles every eight years. In the United States, 9,600 different periodicals are published annually.[2] The current *Ulrich's International Directory of Periodicals* includes nearly 165,000 titles. This is a 71% increase over the number of titles reported in 1980/81 and a 200% increase over 1975.[3]

The price escalation of scholarly writings, particularly in journals, has been equally dramatic. According to statistics gathered annually by the Association of Research Libraries, the increase over the past two decades is over 400%, far in excess of any other measures of national growth: the Consumer Price Index, the Higher Education Price Index, or the level of funding available to research institutions. In the last decade alone, the annual average increase for the serial unit price has been 11.4% and for the monograph unit price 5.9%.[4]

Although most monographs and serials titles are still produced in paper, traditional formats are being augmented by a variety of media and electronic formats. In 1975, the ARL *Statistics* reported data for three formats: monographs, serials, and microforms.[5] In 1995, the *Statistics* report data on the additional formats of: computer files, cartographic materials, graphic materials, audio-visual materials, video/film, government documents, and archives/manuscripts.[6]

The Association of Research Libraries has also monitored the development of electronic journals. New titles are appearing at an amazing rate of 6 to 10 daily. The Association publishes the *Directory of Electronic Journals, Newsletters, and Academic Discussion Lists*, which recently posted 675 electronic journals and newsletters and 2,500 scholarly lists, reflecting an increase in the number of electronic resources of over 140% since the previous edition in 1994 and 4.5 times larger than the 1st edition in July 1991.[7] It is expected that the 1996 Directory will list almost 2000 electronic journals and newsletters. Recognizing the importance of these information resources, research libraries are moving quickly to provide access to them and are establishing a significant market for this relatively new vehicle of scholarly communication.

Another measure of the explosive growth of scholarly materials during this period is the growth in information resources held by the largest research libraries in North America. In 1975, the resources of ARL members in the aggregate included: 230 million volumes, 96 million microforms, and 2.7 million serials.[8] Then, research libraries' annual expenditures exceeded $590 million, with $151 million spent on acquisitions.[9] In 1995, the ARL member collections grew to include almost 415 million volumes, nearly 430 million microforms, and 3.5 million serials.[10] Research libraries' annual expenditures now exceed $ 2.3 billion, of which $648 million is spent on acquisitions.[11]

Yet, while collections in the aggregate have grown significantly during this period, there is evidence that the purchasing power of libraries has declined. Each year, despite rising expenditures, libraries were able to purchase fewer materials than they did the year before. ARL data show for example, that since 1986, ARL libraries doubled expenditures for serials while buying 8% fewer titles. These same data show that during the last decade, ARL libraries reduced the number of monograph purchases by 23%.[12]

An analysis of what research libraries has acquired during the past twenty years also reveals significant shifts in collection management practices. A report by ARL establishes that there has been a steep decline in foreign language acquisitions, a decrease in the percentage of unique titles in many subject areas, and an increased concentration on core materials.[13]

Historically, 40 to 60 percent of materials in many of the major research collections have been foreign imprints. Currently, this appears to have dropped to around 25%. Research libraries have been forced to reduce their long-standing commitment to foreign acquisitions at a time when international research materials are becoming increasingly important to research and economic development. Expansion of the global publishing output, the internationalization of research, and the growing interdependence of national economies have intensified the need for foreign materials even as individual libraries are becoming less able to fulfill that need. As a result, the portion of the world's output of knowledge that is readily made available to the North American student and scholar appears to be diminishing.[14]

Research libraries have mounted multiple responses to cope with these pressures. First, research libraries are turning to regional and local consortia to coordinate the purchase of expensive resources, to rationalize cancellations of serial titles, and to license access to electronic information resources. These consortial arrangements allow libraries to exercise greater influence on the marketplace, leverage local investment for broader access, and save on legal and accounting costs.

Secondly, there is an effort in the educational community to strengthen the consumer's role in understanding and influencing the dynamics of the system. This involves acquainting faculty, administrators, and students with the changes taking place in publishing and scholarly communication and securing their involvement in devising responses. Many efforts are now aimed at informing faculty of the causes and the destructive impacts of the continuing price spiral for scholarly information. These efforts, undertaken by individual research library leaders, as well as the ARL's Office of Scientific and Academic Publishing, are driving the re-examination of the nature of local investment in information resources.

Third, there is the formation of alliances among research libraries, scholarly societies, university presses, and like parties to encourage competition to commercial, high-priced publishers. During this period, calls for the scholarly enterprise to reassert control over its creative products have appeared. One of the most important movements is aimed at establishing a university-based electronic publishing system. Such a system would encourage new partnerships among authors, librarians, and not-for-profit and cost-based publishers to assure the flow and ready availability of scholarly information. It would also take advantage of existing electronic publishing and network capabilities to ensure authenticated databases of scholarly information.

Research libraries continue to be the primary points of access to scholarly information in the emerging information age. Successfully coping with the proliferation of information resources and skyrocketing price increases is one of the phenomenal success stories in higher education for the past twenty years. The leaders of today are exploiting available technologies, engaging the campus community in discussions to shape a new future, and forging imaginative new funding strategies to engage these pressures, combining new sources of financial support with the reallocation of available funds to continue to build significant, diversified repositories of research resources.

Services

During the last twenty years, bibliographic, abstracting, and indexing tools have been strengthened, information services customized, physical access to information streamlined, remote access to required information facilitated, and skilled interpretive services broadened and enriched. Increasingly, the success of a research library is based not only on the number of books and serials in the collection, but also on the effective use of these information resources. Research libraries have turned to innovative and enhanced services to continue to meet the ever expanding information needs and interests of their various constituencies.

These new services embrace electronic document delivery, electronic journals, digitization of library resources, on-demand publishing, and access to network resources. Extension of the research libraries' service capacities marks another notable success of the last two decades. Increasingly, the critical problem is the cost-effectiveness of the various innovative efforts to meet the information requirements of the scholar and the student.

To help provide universal access to widely dispersed collections, research libraries are cooperating with one another in buying, cataloging, storing, and lending research materials. One of the chief means of cooperation is through shared cataloging arrangements. The keystone of the cooperative efforts developed was to find a way to create the original catalog record only once, and then provide these records to other libraries through large computer-based bibliographic utilities such as OCLC, Inc. or by making the on-line catalogs available on the network. OCLC alone has over 34 million catalog records and over 585 million holdings records. [15] Materials that are recorded in these databases can be borrowed through interlibrary loan or can be photocopied and faxed directly to the user. Libraries are rapidly moving on the goal of transmitting full texts directly to users via high-speed computer networks.

Perhaps one of the most astounding accomplishments of this period is the extensive retrospective conversion of library card catalogs to machine readable format and their subsequent transmission via on-line public access catalogs (OPACs). The leader in this respect was the Harvard College Library, which undertook a comprehensive conversion of all existing card catalogs to computerized form. By the end of 1996, the project will be complete and over nine million records will be available in the Harvard on-line library system (HOLLIS). [16] Harvard is one of the first libraries of it size and rank to achieve this goal and it has set a level of achievement that is prompting other large research libraries to commit the money and energy to conversion projects. A recent survey of ARL members, for example, indicates that 95% of research library holdings are available via on-line public access catalogs. [17]

The electronic revolution has transformed both bibliographic and physical access to scholarly information. It is estimated that ARL members are allocating 8 to 14 percent of their materials budgets to electronic information, including document delivery. In the past two decades, new information tools such as CD-ROMs have made library resources more easily accessible to library users, consequently increasing the number of reference questions asked, as well as increasing the general demand for other library services. In the last five years, staff in ARL libraries accommodated increases of 13,000 instructional sessions, almost 10 million additional circulation's, and almost 2 million additional requests for information assistance from students and faculty. [18]

ARL now collects experimental data to provide a sense of the investments research libraries make in electronic services, document delivery, on-line catalogs, public services, and facilities. *The Report on the 1993-94 ARL Supplemental Statistics* indicates that the 108 academic ARL members spent over $59 million on automation ($40 million on computer hardware and software, and slightly over $19 million on bibliographic utilities). In addition, $23 million was spent on electronic information and $4.4 million on document delivery/interlibrary loans. [19]

One illustration of research libraries' determination to manage cost effective access to broadly distributed research collections is the ARL's North American Interlibrary Loan and Document Delivery (NAILDD) Project. This project seeks to promote technical and system developments that improve the identification, ordering, and delivery of materials not owned locally.

The NAILDD project came out of a study of the costs of interlibrary loan that identified the average cost for a complete ILL transaction as approaching $30 in 1993.[20] This figure caused great concern that this access model would be too expensive to maintain, especially in light of the rapid increase in the use of ILL/DD. In the past five years alone, for example, interlibrary borrowing by research libraries has increased by more than 35%.[21] Because of this, research library leaders are putting into place user-centered services in which self-sufficient library users are empowered to choose multiple access modes (novice, expert, independent) to search for, request, and receive materials from a range of sources, including but not limited to local library collections. Electronic communication and the establishment of networks, consortia, and inter-institutional agreements are similarly making the dissemination of information more effective, not only for digitized materials, but also for printed books and photocopies.

Another vexing set of issues faced by research libraries during the past twenty years was copyright. In 1976, a new copyright law was enacted that benefited greatly from the leadership and influence of librarians. This law successfully balanced the intellectual property rights of authors, publishers, and copyright owners with society's need for the free exchange of ideas. For the first time, this law codified a series of practices that are essential to effective learning and research.

Each year, millions of researchers, students, and other members of the public benefit from access to library collections - access that is supported by fair use, the right of libraries to reproduce materials under certain circumstances, and other provisions of the copyright law. These provisions ensure that copyright ownership does not become an absolute monopoly over the distribution of and access to copyrighted information. The continued protection of the fair use, library, and other relevant provisions of the Copyright Act of 1976, and their balanced application in an electronic environment, offer the prospect of better library services, better teaching, and better research without impairing the market for copyrighted material.

The future promises the continued, shifting nature of public services. The increasing availability of electronic information technologies promises to replace traditional venues of collection access with remote access to digitized texts, making materials available to scholars and students immediately. Fundamental to the success of this new paradigm is the reliable availability of at least one fully accessible, archival copy (preferably digitized) of all the publications necessary for research and teaching and the existence of a means (a database, a network and a delivery system) for identifying, locating, and accessing those publications. Assuring that the access rights enjoyed by libraries in the print environment are also enjoyed in the electronic environment is an essential goal if libraries are to realize complete copyright protection in this decade.

Preservation

The preservation of the nation's intellectual heritage is a defining function for research libraries and their host universities. During the last two decades, the importance of preservation achieved sufficient focus and visibility to launch concerted action. A large part of the accomplishments of this period is due to the ability of research library leaders to articulate for society the dimensions of the problem and to define and mount local, regional, and national responses that are now serving to address the preservation problem.

It is estimated that 80 million items, or upwards to one third of the research collections in the United States, are embrittled or are in such condition that the item's next use would result in its destruction due to its printing on acidic paper. This dilemma is being addressed through a multi-faceted approach of traditional and new technologies, physical conservation, reformatting, and preventive measures. Three strategies were developed and implemented to address this brittle book crisis.

The first strategy concerns saving the items threatened with extinction. The Association of Research Libraries, working in concert with the Commission on Preservation and Access and the National Humanities Alliance, promoted a comprehensive plan to save the most endangered scholarly materials. The resulting Brittle Book Program was funded by the U.S. Congress in 1988. The program is operated by the National Endowment for the Humanities (NEH) and targets 3 million items in the humanities for physical reformatting and bibliographic documentation through a national coordinated system. This program, scheduled for twenty years, has already reformatted over 750,000 volumes.

It must be noted that dealing with the brittle book problem is a response to a historical legacy - a preventive strategy is needed for the future. The life expectancy of paper made since 1820 is only 50 to 75 years. Thus, the vast bulk of research collections, as much as 75% of the collections in research libraries, face a slow process of embrittlement over time if action is not taken to de-acidify the paper on which they are printed. The chemical treatment of collections is essential to prevent a future brittle book crisis. Methods for this chemical treatment have been developed or evaluated by the Library of Congress. This period has demonstrated that the process of de-acidifying or stabilizing paper is a cost-effective preservation measure that can significantly increase the longevity of acidic library collections.

Third, scholarly publishers are moving to the use of non-acidic paper for publishing materials of enduring value. University presses have achieved this shift and commercial and government publishers are following. ARL, along with others in the library community, promoted a national policy on permanent paper, and the U.S. Congress passed a resolution in support of this policy. While much has been accomplished domestically to avoid a future preservation problem, there remains the challenge of publications printed overseas.

Beyond the establishment and pursuit of these broad strategies, one of the most important accomplishments during the past twenty years was the development of institutional strategies and programs to address preservation concerns on an ongoing basis. In the eighties, formal preservation programs emerged in research libraries for the first time. These programs go well beyond the binding and maintenance efforts of the past and are configured as distinct administrative units, separately staffed, funded, and administered. According to data collected regularly by ARL, the number of programs managed by a preservation administrator has grown steadily to 92 out of the 119 members by 1994. This development was accompanied by significant growth in preservation expenditures and staffing allocations of the ARL membership. The latest data show an annual expenditure of over $77 million. [22]

A more recent addition to the preservation agenda for research libraries is the flood of information made available in electronic formats. The preservation of this information for future users requires understanding the limitations of the software and hardware. In fact, parallel use of all these strategies and aggressive development of new technologies must be undertaken to ensure preservation not just of older materials, but of the constant stream of new ones in print, graphic, electronic, and other forms, as well. The single greatest challenge in addressing the preservation of all research resources, especially electronic resources, is not technology based, but is the need for purposeful engagement of questions surrounding the collective management of intellectual property for the benefit of the scholarly enterprise.

Technology

Improvements in information access and organizational performance through the automation of library functions and the use of advanced telecommunication networks is rapidly leading toward the concept of distributed digital research libraries of the 21st century. Integrating electronic information services into the traditional library was another accomplishment of the last two decades.

Inventories of efforts to automate the major functions of research libraries demonstrate a rapid movement during the past twenty years toward highly automated research organizations. As noted earlier, all ARL members have on-line public access catalogs and most have completed a retrospective conversion of their bibliographic records. Libraries are also providing their constituencies with access to digital information throughout the world via the National Information Infrastructure (NII).

An explosion of opportunities in information technology, electronic media, and networked information is occurring. The increased availability of computers and computer networks is revolutionizing the way students and scholars research, learn, access information, and publish. Libraries are responding by orchestrating traditional library activities in new ways and creating new activities to fit this altered universe of learning and research.

Library catalogs and campus-wide information systems represent important networked information resources, and it is library resources that account for the lion's share of the growth and excitement in contemporary networking. Redesigning local library information systems in order to benefit from networked information resources and services is underway as campuses are rewired to use networked information. Research libraries have up-graded the information technology capabilities of their staff and have undertaken training to ensure that end-users are skilled and well-prepared to use new services.

One of the most noteworthy accomplishments of research library leaders in the last decade is the establishment of The Coalition for Networked Information (CNI). CNI was formed by ARL, CAUSE, and EDUCOM to create a partnership among technology and library associations to collectively promote the successful deployment of telecommunication networks to improve scholarly productivity. During its six years of operation, the Coalition has played a major role in exploring network applications, encouraging the exchange of information about the use of networks, and addressing the problems and obstacles faced by those advancing scholarship and intellectual productivity through the effective use of networked information.

Many research libraries are experimenting with the digital library concept and a variety of collaborative projects are underway to explore the potential of digital libraries. These virtual libraries will provide databases of primary research and education materials, as well as secondary materials that will provide reference information about the contents of print and digital collections. Because of the extraordinary advances in communications technology, it is becoming progressively easier to connect the research and education communities to each other and to the growing variety of research resources and services to which they contribute and on which they depend. For example, sixteen public and academic institutions, including the Library of Congress, are participating in the National Digital Library Federation. This program focuses on American history and culture, with the aim of building a global digital library. Databases of primary research and education materials, known as "digital libraries", and of secondary materials that provide reference information about the contents of print collections, as well as of the contents of digital libraries, are beginning to appear on research and education networks, and the rate at which they will continue to appear promises to accelerate exponentially.

It is obvious that expenditures and funding for automation and electronic delivery of information are now solidly part of normal library operations and the annual operating budget. They are no longer part of some special experiment or some one-time, grant-supported project. This is a fundamental policy and leadership strategy designed to meet the challenges of the technology boom of the last two decades.

Research institutions, including their libraries, are moving toward an electronic infrastructure that has the potential scope and scale of many existing physical infrastructures, such as road and water systems. This new electronic infrastructure will both stimulate and constrain our activities and aspirations in the same way that these other types of infrastructures have throughout modern history. The best strategy for making use of these investments in computers and networks are collaborative and national, not individual and local. More than ever before, we need to work out collaborative strategies for institutions and individuals to share knowledge with one another. Virtual libraries and distributed information networks hold the best promise of the future.

Management

This has been a turbulent period for the management of research libraries. Research library leaders actively sought approaches for reducing staff-intensive activities while improving the cost effectiveness of the services and resources they offered. One indication of this accomplishment is found in the annual statistics gathered by ARL. At the end of 1995, these data indicate an increasing investment in information technology,[23] a continuing challenge in maintaining collections under adverse economic trends,[24] and a decline in staffing levels.[25]

It is worth noting that while staff size grew during the seventies, it stabilized in the eighties. During these years, the ratio of student assistants to permanent professional and support staff rose: as if ARL libraries were restraining staffing costs by increasingly hiring less expensive personnel. The most recent ARL *Statistics* describe a decline in staff size over the last five years.[26]

During this five-year period, a variety of management strategies were adopted by research libraries. A study of research library management practices in 1992 revealed that virtually every library explored some form of internal restructuring via consolidating units, eliminating functions, abolishing managerial jobs, or substituting part-time professionals. Most libraries report eliminated positions over the last few years.[27] Given these demographic trends, the reoccurrence of hiring freezes, staff contractions, and internal re-structuring, it is apparent that current staff need to be developed to meet changing needs.

A major investment was made by research library leaders in the development of the management skills of academic librarians. ARL established the Office of Management Services (OMS) in 1970, and, over the twenty five years of operation, this office has delivered a variety of management and leadership training programs, organizational development programs, and a systems and procedures exchange center. The office has focused its efforts on bringing new and emerging management concepts into academic and research library management. An underlying assumption in the development of programs at OMS is that one way of strengthening organizational performance is by developing the competence of the individuals within the organization.

One measure of the success of the OMS is the extent of its exposure to the staff of research libraries. Almost all member libraries have employed one or more of the organizational services of the OMS, and almost all of the senior leadership in research libraries today have had one or more developmental experiences provided by the OMS framework.[28]

The past twenty years seen produced a new level of commitment to training and staff development. Because skills and knowledge must be updated as change and innovation are introduced, a positive attitude toward continuous, lifelong learning has been, and must continue to be, encouraged and fostered. Research libraries also have developed stronger in-house training capabilities to take an active role in the systematic development of library staff.

Also during these two decades, soliciting increasing revenue from outside funds, gifts, grants, and fees for services has been a significant management strategy adopted by most institutions. Half of the U.S. public institutions, for example, have or are developing a foundation affiliated with the library or the university for fund-raising purposes.[29] These efforts in external fund development by public institutions mirror the historical accomplishments of private institutions.

A significant shift in the age of research library professionals has also occurred during the last five years. This is outlined in Stanley Wilder's *The Age Demographics of Academic Librarians: A Profession Apart*, which identifies dramatic changes impacting the academic and research library community. This study notes that, as a group, academic librarians are older than members of most comparable professions, and the group is getting older. Wilder suggests that 16 percent of the 1995 ARL population will retire by 2000. Another 16 percent will retire between 2000 and 2005, and 24 percent between 2010 and 2020 and a large portions of the research library staff will retire over the next 25 years. Wilder points out that losing a high percentage of ARL's population to retirement will result in a critical loss of experience.[30]

An example of this is the rate of turnover currently being experienced in ARL directorships. Out of the 119 member libraries, there are over 20 directorships currently open. This rate of turnover is comparable to the dramatic change in leadership that occurred two decades ago and heralds a generational shift in leadership.

In 1990, the OMS began a fresh effort to help libraries respond to the changing demographics of the workplace. Pressure to increase cultural diversity in the workplace by hiring minorities in professional positions was building, and with money from the H.W. Wilson Foundation, the OMS Diversity Program was established. Over the past five years, this program has served broadly as a resource to the profession by eliciting and sharing information on effective approaches to recruiting and retaining a diverse workforce.

The changing nature of the work and staff of academic and research libraries increases the urgency for greater experimentation with new organizational structures. The values and needs of a new generation of staff are no longer met by the bureaucratic and hierarchical structures that were used in the past. Matrix organizations and self-managed work teams will better suit the more integrated, project nature of work in today's libraries. A wave of library reorganizations is underway, all aimed at developing organizations more capable of rapid, innovative response to their environment. A desire for greater voice and participation, and a more politically sophisticated and knowledgeable staff, will compel libraries to continue to move toward more decentralized budgets and operations.

Concurrently, libraries are successfully exploring the application of various qualitative and quantitative techniques to improve productivity and performance. Library leaders have demonstrated agility in adapting to the new environment of higher education, government policy, and public and private funding. Budgetary pressures, combined with the skyrocketing costs of library operation, prompt library leaders to experiment with new organizational and technical aspects of managing operations, including processes for initiating and managing change, and measuring and modeling costs and performance.

The past twenty years has seen an increasing awareness of the complexity of academic and research libraries as organizations. As the competition for resources, both within the library and externally as part of the university, becomes more intense, the ability to observe, diagnose and take action becomes more important. Sound planning and decision-making skills become essential for financial support, demonstrating accountability, evaluating operations, and measuring effectiveness.

The challenge of the future will be to find ways of dealing with the familiar old problems and meeting the provocative changes caused by new user demands. User and provider expectations, new information technologies, new staff values and expectations regarding the work environment, and new organizational structures are all beginning to emerge from these refinements. Ongoing investment in human resources continues to be a key success factor in assuring organizational effectiveness.

It has become clear over the past two decades that it will be a long time before we can expect another period of relative stability. Economics, demographics, and technology will continually reshape the landscape for libraries. Management will be driven by the need to respond effectively to constant change from both within and outside libraries.

Closure

Historically, North American research libraries have enjoyed a steady growth in collections and expansions of services. During the last two decades, these same institutions have faced an interruption in this growth because of a decrease in the proportion of university funding directed to them. This decline in university funding was paralleled by a decline in the external funds available from the federal government and private foundations, and a skyrocketing in the price of information resources.

Simultaneously, an explosion of opportunities in information technology, electronic media, and networked information has occurred. The increased availability of computers and computer networks is revolutionizing the way students and scholars research, learn, access information, and publish. Research libraries are striving to stay abreast of applications for these new forms of information access and use.

This is a period of extraordinary change which provides interest and challenge. As we look to the future, redefining the research library in an electronic information environment challenges us to attract new investments and operating funds, while pursuing the core mission of research libraries to provide equitable access to the record of human existence and accomplishment.

The traditional skills we have developed in building access to information resources are being reconceptualized. We are working toward a future information system that brings together the library, the university press, the book store, the media center, and the emerging electronic institutional database into a single developing network. New ways of strengthening research libraries' performance and capabilities are being developed. New efforts are being explored to introduce and effectively utilize multiple forms of electronic information. Alliances are linking research libraries with other agencies in higher education to shape a hospitable future environment for scholarly communication.

The precise outcome of this period of experimentation is not predictable except to say that libraries and universities are being transformed. We are moving quickly to where new technologies secure significant cost savings while enhancing access to required information resources. We hope the next 20 years will be as productive and exciting as the last two decades as library leaders help create, invent, and proactively shape this future.

Notes

1. Cummings, introduction.

2. Wurman, introduction.

3. Popilskis, preface.

4. Kyrillidou, 1996, p. 11.

5. Frankie, p. 34.

6. Kyrillidou, 1996, pp. 23-27.

7. King, p. 15.

8. Frankie, p. 30.

9. Frankie, p. 37.

10. Kyrillidou, 1996, p. 28-29.

11. Kyrillidou, 1996, p. 36- 37.

12. Kyrillidou, 1996, p. 11.

13. Reed-Scott, 1996, p. 62-63.

14. Ibid.

15. Dean, p. 8.

16. Berry, p. 30.

17. Kyrillidou, 1995, p. 3.

18. Kyrillidou, 1996, p. 9.

19. Kyrillidou, 1995, p. 2.

20. Roche, p. iv.

21. Kyrillidou, 1996, p. 8.

22. Reed-Scott, 1995, pp. 11 & 14.

23. Kyrillidou, 1995, p. 5.

24. Kyrillidou, 1996, p. 10.

25. Ibid, p. 8.

26. Ibid.

27. Melville, p. vii.

28. Jurow and Webster, p. 141.

29. Melville, p. 10.

30. Wilder, p. 40.

References

ARL Policy Manual. Washington, DC: Association of Research Libraries, 1995.

ARL Program Plan, 1995. Washington, DC: Association of Research Libraries, 1995.

Berry, John. "Departing Shots form Richard De Gennaro." *Library Journal*, November 15, 1995.

Cummings, Anthony M. et al. *University Libraries and Scholarly Communication. A Study Prepared for The Andrew W. Mellon Foundation.* Washington, DC: Association of Research Libraries, 1992.

Dean, Nita, ed. OCLC *Newsletter, January/February 1996*. Dublin, OH: OnLine Computer Library Center, 1996.

Frankie, Suzanne, ed. *ARL Statistics*, 1975- 1976. Washington, DC: Association of Research Libraries, 1977.

Jurow, Susan and Duane Webster. Promoting Management Excellence in Research Libraries Through Training and Staff Development. *Library Administration and Management*, Summer 1990.

King, Lizabeth, ed. *The Directory of Electronic Journals, Newsletters and Academic Discussion Lists*, 5th ed. Washington, DC: Association of Research Libraries, 1995.

Kyrillidou, Martha, ed. *ARL Statistics, 1994 - 1995.* Washington, DC: Association of Research Libraries, 1996.

Kyrillidou, Martha, ed. *Report on the 1993-94 ARL Supplementary Statistics*. Washington, DC: Association of Research Libraries, 1995.

Melville, Annette. *Resource Strategies for the 90's: Trends in ARL University Libraries, Occasional Paper #16*. Washington, DC: Association of Research Libraries, 1994.

Popilskis, Edvika, ed. et al. *Ulrich's International Periodicals Directory, 34th Edition, 1996* New Providence, NJ: R.R. Bowker 1995.

Reed-Scott, Jutta, ed. *ARL Preservation Statistics, 1993-94*. Washington, DC: Association of Research Libraries, 1995.

Reed-Scott, Jutta. *Scholarship, Research Libraries and Global Publishing*. Washington, DC: Association of Research Libraries, 1996.

Roche, Marilyn. *ARL/RLG Interlibrary Loan Cost Study*. Washington, DC: Association of Research Libraries, 1993.

Webster, Duane. *Promoting the Principles of Copyright: ARL: Bimonthly Newsletter of Research Library Issues and Actions, #169.* Washington, D.C.: Association of Research Libraries, July 1993.

Wilder, Stanley J. *The Age Demographics of Academic Librarians: A Profession Apart*. Washington, DC: Association of Research Libraries, 1996.

Wurman, Richard. *Information Anxiety: What To Do When Information Doesn't Tell You What You Need To Know*. New York: Bantam Books, 1990.

The University Library in a Collaboratorium:

by Robert Wedgeworth

In the spring of 1968 volume 1, number 1 of the *Journal of Library Automation* appeared including an article by Richard De Gennaro, "The Development and Administration of Automated Systems in Academic Libraries." The journal, edited by Frederick G. Kilgour, heralded the establishment of a new specialization in the library field. Indeed, the Information Science and Automation Division (ISAD) of the American Library Association, later the Library and Information Technology Association (LITA), was founded at the ALA Annual Conference of 1968. De Gennaro's contribution was a carefully crafted, thoughtful overview of the development of library automation in academic libraries that was to characterize his writings on the subject for the next two and a half decades.[1] This essay will revisit some of the major points of that article with the perspective of almost thirty years of experience. It will also suggest a model for research library development in the years to come.

Approaches to Library Automation

By the end of the 1960's the engine of rapid change in libraries had picked up momentum fueled by the growth of higher education, the availability of new computer-based technologies and an infectious enthusiasm for the use of new technologies in libraries. Against this background De Gennaro projected a scenario for the development of library automation in academic libraries comprised of three modes: "wait for developments approach," "direct approach to a total system," and "the evolutionary approach to a total system." The most prominent advocate for the "wait for developments approach" was the late William S. "Bill" Dix, University Librarian at Princeton, who argued eloquently that the risks involved in adopting what were clearly exploratory and experimental techniques were too great for all but the very large libraries. Most of the library community, according to Dix, should wait for this pioneering stage to be completed and then build upon proven results.[2]

Yale University Library, whose library automation effort had been led by Fred Kilgour until his move to the Ohio College Library Center (later OCLC) in 1967, along with the libraries at the University of Chicago, Florida Atlantic University and Stanford University were the most prominent advocates for the "direct approach to a total system". They were the pioneers in the library-centered approach to a total systems design. This was an exceedingly ambitious course of action given that the libraries adopting it had to build the capacity to develop and execute the design as they were planning it. These systems were the conceptual models for the integrated library systems that developed later.[3]

De Gennaro and the Harvard University Libraries were the most prominent example of the "evolutionary approach to a total system," which was an effort to reduce uncertainty to a series of calculated risks in developing library sub-systems successively while building resources and staff capabilities to support an automated library system. This was popular with many libraries which could only afford to develop slowly. It became the preferred approach, however, due to the development of library networks which allowed groups of libraries to create computer-based catalogs and other cooperative services on a very economical scale.

Initially, library automation efforts focused on cataloging, circulation, and, to a lesser extent, acquisitions. Kilgour had moved to Ohio to establish the Ohio College Library Center (OCLC) in 1967. Its purpose was to build a cooperative computer-based catalog serving the needs of all of the academic libraries in the State and thereby increase efficiency by reducing the need to duplicate repetitive tasks. The immediate success of OCLC attracted libraries outside the state of Ohio to clamor to join the cooperative cataloging scheme and by 1978 had spawned a whole series of state and regional networks of libraries of all types which pooled their resources in order to benefit from the development of an on-line cataloging system. Some of these networks were led by strong state libraries like the Washington State Library (WLN) or the Illinois State Library (ILLINET). Others emerged from strong regional ties like NELINET in New England and SOLINET in the southeastern part of the nation. Most were multi-type library systems that brought together academic, special, public, and, often, school libraries for common purposes. Network agencies were created that contracted with OCLC, and later other firms, to deliver services to the members via the network or directly. Network administration of contracts provided a single point of contact for multiple libraries thus keeping contract renewal and maintenance costs low.

Access to an on-line MARC record file augmented by a growing file of locally produced records of the OCLC member libraries was the major attraction of OCLC and quickly replaced the practice of ordering catalog cards produced by the Library of Congress. Although most libraries had not committed to an on-line local catalog, the announcement in 1975 that the Library of Congress was considering closing its catalog by 1980 encouraged many libraries to begin to explore alternatives to the card catalog including book catalogs and computer output microform catalogs that were becoming popular with public libraries due to their low costs for replication in many locations.

The incremental approach to library automation was supported further by the advent of commercial services beginning in the 1970's that developed automated catalog and circulation systems for the library market. CLSI, Inc. led the initial efforts to create a library market for circulation systems. At the same time, many libraries were developing home-grown circulation systems with available technologies and local personnel. The focus on the cataloging and circulation functions defined library automation well into the 1980's when the growing popularity of on-line databases of bibliographic and other information sources began to take effect.

Beginning in the mid 1970's several hundred new on-line databases began to appear each year. Although initially their content was scientific, led by the National Library of Medicine's MEDLINE, and Dialog, Inc., databases in law, accounting and other professional and academic fields followed quickly. While most of these databases were indexes and abstracts to published journal literature, some began to offer direct information to the user like TOXLINE, the on-line file of known toxic substances and their antidotes. The leading users of on-line databases of all types were law firms, government agencies and universities.

Although library automation in academic libraries developed incrementally, as projected by De Gennaro, the reasons had more to do with the traditions of library cooperation through newly developed networks and the gradual expansion of the library market to include automated services than with a calculated strategy. However, his concerns for monitoring the costs of library automation, for the building staff capability and for the organization of systems departments in libraries continue to be major administrative issues in academic library management.

Management of Library Automation

In the early days of library automation there were no systems specialists in libraries. Graduate library education programs offered little, if any, systems and computer training, therefore, early systems specialists were either self-taught or brought into librarianship from engineering, computational physics and related fields. One of the first major efforts to acquaint librarians with computers and systems development was initiated by Joseph Becker and Bob Hayes as part of the World's Fair project in Seattle in 1962. Librarians selected to work in an exhibit entitled "Library 21" were treated to a two week orientation and training course on basic computing, reprography and systems analysis taught by Bob Hayes. Becker was an engineer and consultant to a number of government agencies who had a wide acquaintance with libraries. Hayes was a UCLA Professor of mathematics and computer science who became so interested in the problems of libraries and librarians that he became Dean of the library school at UCLA. The World's Fair project was so successful that it continued for two more years in New York and trained almost two hundred librarians.

As the graduate library schools moved slowly to respond to the need for library automation specialists, the academic libraries identified the talent already available, instituted training programs in computing and systems analysis assisted by the networks, and attracted capable staff from other disciplines within the institution. If the 1970's was the decade of the rise of library networks, the 1980's was the decade of crisis in library education. Although there remained more than fifty accredited graduate library and information science programs, the schools were uncertain about their future and their impact on the field.[4] The student bodies, though talented, were largely self-selected with only minimal efforts to broaden the pool of applicants and thereby increase competition for the limited number of admissions available each year. The faculties were small in comparison to other university programs for professional education and the schools were under-funded for the range of technologies they needed to maintain in order to reflect the current state of professional practice. In their efforts to overcome these obstacles using external funds to accelerate change, they were shunted from one priority to another by well-meaning government officials and foundation officers. On a much smaller scale, the situation for graduate library education was similar to that of graduate schools of education described by Derek Bok in his 1985-86 annual report as President of Harvard University.[5]

The relationship of the crisis in library education to the development of library automation and the advance of other information technologies is a subtle one that needs more thorough exploration than is possible here. However, it should be noted that the pressures to reduce the size of higher education in the 1980's in contrast to the heady expansion in the 1960's put many small academic and professional fields at risk. The negative impact of those pressures on graduate library education programs reflected another dimension of the question of whether librarians or computer specialists should lead the development of computer-based library and information services. Those same funding pressures limited the possibilities for the expansion of technical specialties in library staffing. Yale University was the first major academic library to create a Research and Development unit. A number of libraries had some specialized systems staff by the beginning of the 1980's, but few kept a specific interest in research beyond the development of current systems.

The problems associated with library automation developments of the past three decades outlined so well by De Gennaro in 1968 lead naturally toward speculation about what the next few decades will mean for libraries. Integrated local library systems connected to a wide range of external information sources is now a reality for many academic libraries. However, strategy, organization and costs will continue to challenge approaches to academic library development.

A New Challenge

It is within the tradition of academic institutions for a faculty member to ask a student of the humanities to describe the characteristics of the Italian Renaissance. However, it is now feasible for a faculty member to ask a student to recreate the environment of the Italian Renaissance in its philosophy, sights and sounds. The question is what role will academic libraries play in supporting the teaching and research programs that require access to multimedia information sources that can combine audio, full motion video and text?

The Digital Library

Throughout most of this century academic libraries have concentrated on developing on-site collections of materials that support the teaching and research programs of their parent institution, housing the collections in buildings specifically designed to optimize storage and use, and developing systems to provide access to the contents of these collections. Each of these developments, in most cases, had required that libraries acquire physical artifacts, catalog, organize and store them in specific locations. Users, on the other hand, were required to go physically to the location of libraries, identify items needed through the use of the catalog and physically retrieve items for their use. Increasingly, it is feasible, with the use of computer workstations, on-line telecommunications and digitized files of text, sound and video, to accomplish all of the foregoing tasks from a single location, following the advice of Nicholas Negroponte " to move bits instead of atoms."[6] This development called the "digital library" or "the virtual library" represents not just a conceptual change in how libraries operate, but also a change in what is considered to be "scholarly information." For our purposes here, the digital library comprises one or more organized files of digitized information that can be accessed locally or remotely for search, display or transmittal. The virtual library is a concept that assumes the existence of one or more digital libraries.

Thanks to the ubiquity of the World Wide Web technology, all over the world experiments are being conducted and prototypical production processes are being initiated to digitize files of information for storage, retrieval, display and transmittal. These technologies take us well beyond the concept of library automation, but the managerial issues of strategy, personnel, costs and organization continue to be a challenge. Although existing files of documents, images and other materials of interest to specific audiences (art images, laws, classic works of literature) are targets for digitization, the race is on to develop files of new materials for which users will be willing to pay for access. Prominent among these are current scientific and technical journals.

Images of scientific journal articles have been available in full text for some time on an experimental basis from publishers like Elsevier. These are "bit-mapped" images of journal pages that can be stored, retrieved and displayed as whole pages. Few journal publishers have approached the task of producing searchable full text as it requires a labor intensive process of technical editing, the cost of which is daunting even to technological giants like OCLC. For scientific materials there are other technical problems that must be overcome. Currently, there is no way to display mathematics accurately and consistently except as an image which cannot be searched. Also, publishers vary so widely in the way they describe their documents in digital format that it inhibits the efficiency of large scale search and retrieval systems. The full deployment of a digital library requires a combination of expertise and technical capability that is only commonly available in universities. However, most universities lack the financial resources to launch such ventures. It is, therefore, highly likely that the initial development of digital libraries in universities will result from complex collaborative ventures.

The Collaboratorium

Several models for digital libraries are under development under the Digital Library Initiative (DLI) sponsored by the National Science Foundation (NSF), NASA and ARPA. The participating universities that are funded to research aspects of the digital library of the future are University of California, Berkeley, University of California, Santa Barbara, Carnegie Mellon, Illinois, Michigan and Stanford. At Illinois, a library-centered collaboratorium is under development that shows promise of interest here. The University Library and the National Center for Supercomputing Applications have come together with researchers from the Graduate School of Library and Information Science, Computer Science, Sociology and Economics to create a digital library in the field of engineering. The University Library is building the testbed of journal articles contributed by a number of engineering and computer science societies. NCSA, creators of MOSAIC, is supporting the software design while the researchers study the architecture of the system, its usability as a search and retrieval tool, the behavior of the users and the economics of making the materials available.

As the center for the acquisition and use of the scholarly record, academic libraries can build similar collaboratoria on other campuses to develop digital libraries. Publishers will not be expected to donate their materials to the digital library of the future. However, we do expect that a wider range of terms and conditions for gaining access to these materials will emerge. Given the decline in journal subscriptions by libraries and the prices announced for electronic journals, it is clear that some alternatives to the current system of discounted individual subscriptions and relatively high price institutional subscriptions must be found. Flexibility is the key. The ability for groups of libraries to subscribe to information sources like electronic journals and pay a rate that is based on the size of the user population and/or the number of simultaneous users is becoming more common. For certain materials it may be feasible for individual institutions to buy articles or access on demand even if the costs are higher than subscriptions.

The collaboratorium creates a transitional mechanism to experiment with many complex arrangements that may define future relationships among libraries, publishers, researchers, students and others. Complex local networks on campuses using sophisticated gateway software requires greater systems staff capability than most academic libraries can possibly afford to maintain. On the other hand, academic computing centers will be increasingly overburdened by the need to teach new applications software while introducing new users to the local network. The convergence of these structural roles is a fundamental reason for considering a collaboratorium approach. Funding staff capability and rapidly obsolescent hardware and software is also a responsibility that needs to be shared among a number of campus entities. Faculty interest in the tools for teaching and research will focus naturally on disciplinary-specific tools and methods, but the fundamental infrastructure will be essential building blocks for the work of their students. Common interests and converging roles are the basis for the concept of a collaboratorium that brings together libraries, academic computing, media centers and faculty who are early implementers of new systems. A common administrative structure may or may not be necessary. However, a formal mechanism for collaborative decision-making will be. At Illinois, a Campus-wide Committee on Communications Technology coordinates major policy decisions related to strategy, funding, training and basic infrastructure for computing and communications technology. The University Library, NCSA, CCSO (academic computing), AISS (administrative computing), Student Services and a Faculty representative comprise the membership of the committee chaired by the Vice Chancellor for Research. The advent of the digital library places academic libraries at the center of the system for campus access to networked information. Four tasks are fundamental to the success of the digital library, and academic libraries have experience and expertise to contribute to each of them. They are: user education, access tools, file management and file maintenance.

User Education

Neither students nor faculty can be presumed to arrive on campuses with a innate knowledge of how to use interactive, complex digital libraries in combination with more traditional materials. As academic computing centers and teaching departments become more involve in deploying hardware and software for specific applications, there will be a major need for a user education function that can be both an introduction to the systems and services available as well as a source of assistance when various problems arise. Academic libraries are especially suited for assuming some of this responsibility given their facilities, information resources and staff expertise in working with users. Students can also be organized by libraries to provide peer training. The library enjoys the advantage of a non-threatening atmosphere where the user will not be graded on their progress, and it is available more hours than many other facilities.

Several years ago at a symposium on higher education and libraries organized at Columbia University the participants comprised largely of faculty and administrators recognized the need to involve the academic library more actively in the teaching and learning programs, but their question was, " ...what will libraries teach?" The July/August 1987 issue of CHANGE gives a summary of the symposium and offers some examples of how widely different institutions as Earlham College, St. Louis Community College and the University of California, Berkeley have involved their libraries in the instructional program.[7]

Access Tools

Columnist Mike Royko of the *Chicago Tribune* described being on the Internet like "driving a car through a blizzard without windshield wipers or lights, and all of the road signs are written upside and backwards. And if you stop and ask someone for help, they stutter in Albanian."[8] If librarians thought users were confused trying to decipher the mysteries of the dictionary card catalog, we cannot begin to imagine the perplexities that will arise as we become more and more dependent on the Internet to provide access to primary teaching, learning and research materials. Poorly organized files, non-standard or non-existent indexing and unedited text are common problems associated with Internet sources. The experience and expertise of libraries and librarians in creating and maintaining standards for organizing information is currently being recognized. The concepts of indexing, abstracting, cross-referencing and cataloging take on new meaning in association with dynamic, world-wide information sources. For example, bibliographical information used to described elements of a printed record can be extracted and stored separately from the digitized text just like a separate bibliography. These files are being referred to as "metadata" files that describe the content and structure of digital documents. Librarians familiar with the MARC record readily recognize some of the elements in these files as author records, title records, reference records, or illustration records.

If we project that the structure of digital information sources will evolve into a series of single and composite document repositories linked to metadata files to facilitate access to their content, we can appreciate the need for libraries and librarians to be actively involved in the design of such a system.

File Management and Maintenance

After a system of repositories of digitized documents, images and other records becomes a reality managing and maintaining them will be the key to effective search and retrieval. Information is dynamic and terms used to refer to certain phenomena this year cannot be assured of currency in the next. Updating files, restructuring files, adding links to relevant information are all tasks with which librarians are familiar in another mode. Libraries themselves are likely to be the home of many repositories of locally produced information sources made available to others via telecommunications. Formulating standards according to protocols established by international standards organizations can be an important regulatory mechanism for Internet sources that is also familiar to librarians.

The Human Side of the Enterprise

The North American library community developed great libraries before it recognized the requirements of specialized personnel to manage them. Its leadership of the organized library world is based not on the generosity of those who have financed the development of great collections and buildings to house them, nor on the absence of wars that have devastated libraries of Europe and elsewhere. The principal basis for the leadership of the North American library community is the community of professionally educated librarians and information specialists who share a similar understanding of the values, techniques and services that characterize our institutions and organizations. It enables us to organize large complex cooperative activities involving individuals and groups widely separated geographically. It motivates us to ensure that those of limited means have some of the same opportunities for learning as those more generously endowed.

Academic libraries are almost by nature collaborative enterprises, and it is that attribute that is likely to be most important in making a successful transition to a digital library environment.

Notes

1.   De Gennaro, Richard. "The Development and Administration of Automated Systems in Academic Libraries." *Journal of Library Automation* 1:1 (1968): 75-91.

2.   Dix, William S. *Annual Report of the Librarian for the Year Ending June 30, 1966.* Princeton: Princeton University Library, 1966.

3.   Kilgour, Frederick G. "Comprehensive Modern Library Systems." *The Brasenose Conference on the Automation of Libraries, Proceedings.* London: Mansell, 1967. pp. 46-56.

4.   *ALA Yearbook.* Edited by Robert Wedgeworth. Chicago: ALA Publishing, 1976-1985.

5.   Bok, Derek. *The President's Report, 1985-86.* Cambridge, MA: Harvard UP, 1987.

6.   Negroponte, Nicholas. *Being Digital.* New York: Knopf, 1995.

7.   Breivik, Patricia Senn. "Making the Most of Libraries." *Change* 19:4 (1987): 44-52.

8.   Royko, Mike. "$126 Million Ranks as Expensive Date." *Chicago Tribune* (February 10, 1994): 3A.

PERSONAL:

1926:	Born, New Haven, CT
1953:	Married Birgit M. Erikson Children: Ralph, George, Christina

MILITARY SERVICE AND RELATED WORK:

1942-1946: U.S. Navy, World War II Pacific, USS Montpelier and USS San Juan. Achieved the rank of Radioman First Class and was awarded ten battle stars and a Navy Unit Commendation.

1952-1953: Employed by Atlas Constructors to build strategic air bases in French Morocco

EDUCATION:

1951: Wesleyan University, CT: B.A. Government

1951,1954: University of Paris (Sorbonne): Cours de Civilisation Francaise

1954: Institut de Phonetique (Paris): Certificat

1951-1955: Universities of Poitiers, Barcelona, Madrid, and Perugia: various language, literature, and history programs.

1956: Columbia University, School of Library Service: M.S. in Library Science

1960: Wesleyan University, CT: M.A. Liberal Studies

1971: Harvard University, Business School: 60th Advanced Management Program

PROFESSIONAL EMPLOYMENT:

1956-1958: New York Public Library Special Recruit Program; Reference Librarian: Economics, Science, and Technology Division; Main Information Desk, and the American History Division.

1958-1970: Harvard University Library Assistant Reference Librarian (1958-1961) Administrative Assistant (1961-1963) Assistant Director (1963-1964) Assistant University Librarian (1964-1966) Associate University Librarian for Systems Development (1966-1969) Senior Associate University Librarian (1969-1970)

1970-1986: University of Pennsylvania, Director of Libraries and Adjunct Professor of English

1987-1990: New York Public Library Director

1990-1996: Harvard University, Roy E. Larsen Librarian of Harvard College

PROFESSIONAL ASSOCIATIONS/ ORGANIZATIONS:

American Library Association (Life Member)

1967-1971: Book Catalogs Committee

1968-1970: Library Technology Program. Advisory Committee

| **1970-1971:** | President: Information Science and Automation Division |
| **1982:** | International Relations Committee |

American Society for Information Science

| **1969:** | Chairman: Special Interest Group on Library Automation and Networks |

Association of Research Libraries

1968-1971:	Microform Technology Project, Consultative Panel
1972-1975:	Management Commission
1973-1974:	Committee on Machine-Readable Data Bases
1973-1976:	Board of Directors
1974-1976:	Task Force on Future of Card Catalogs
1975:	President
1976-1977:	ARL/CRL Joint Committee on a National Periodical Library
1982-1984:	Office of Management Studies. Advisory Committee

Research Libraries Group, Inc.

1979-1989:	Board of Governors
1982-1984:	Chairman: Computer Systems Committee
1982-1985:	Strategic Planning Committee
1982-1986:	Executive Committee
1984-1985:	Chairman: Board of Governors
1993-1996:	Board of Directors
1996:	Chairman: Nominating Committee

OTHER SELECTED PROFESSIONAL ACTIVITIES:

1965-1972:	Committee on Library Automation (COLA)
1966:	Anglo-American Conference on Mechanization of Library Services (Brasenose Conference), Oxford University
1966-1968:	Institute of Electrical and Electronics Engineers (IEEE). Information Advisory Committee
1967:	Conference on the Impact of Technology on the Library Building, Educational Facilities Laboratories
1967-1968:	Principal Investigator Implementing the MARC Project Input System in the Harvard University Library. National Science Foundation (Grant GN-598)
1969:	University of Maryland. Library Administrators Development Program
1969-1970:	Stanford University. BALLOTS External Advisory Committee
1969-1971:	Library of Congress. RECON Working Task Force
1970-1975:	Union Library Catalogue of Pennsylvania. Board and Executive Committee
1973-1976:	Northeast Academic Science Information Center Advisory Board
1975:	Delegate: Japan-US Conference on Libraries and Information Science in Higher Education, 3rd, Kyoto
1975-1979:	PALINET Board and Executive Committee
1976-1977:	OCLC Advisory Council

1977-1979:	National Academy of Science/ National Research Council. Committee on International Scientific and Technical Programs
1977-1981:	Center for Research Libraries Board of Directors
1978:	National Commission on Libraries and Information Science. Advisory Committee on a National Periodicals System
1981:	Frontiers Conference on Future of Research Libraries, UCLA, Lake Arrowhead,CA
1981-1984:	Universal Serials and Book Exchange Board of Directors
1982:	Conference on Online Catalogs, Aspen Institute, Wye Plantation, MD (Sponsored by CLR)
1982:	Wingspread Conference on Research Libraries, Racine, WI (Sponsored by CLR)
1986:	U.S. and Japanese Libraries in Higher Education: the Binational Experience, Tokyo, August 24, 1986. Invited to deliver paper at the symposium.
1988:	US-USSR Seminar on Access to Library Resources through Technology and Preservation, Washington, DC, July 5-8, 1988. Keynote speaker.
1989-1990:	Commission on Preservation and Access
1993-:	Andrew W. Mellon Foundation Advisory Committee
1995-:	Andrew W. Mellon Foundation. JSTOR ("Journal Storage") Board of Trustees

TEACHING AND OTHER ACADEMIC EXPERIENCES:

1968-1969:	Visiting Professor: University of Southern California. Graduate Library School. Institute for the Education and Training of Information Science Faculty. (Funded by USOE)
1978:	Visiting Scholar: University Center, Atlanta, Georgia
1979:	Visiting Distinguished Lecturer: University of British Columbia. School of Librarianship
1980-1981:	Visiting Senior Fellow: Research Libraries Group, Inc., Stanford University. (Forward Planning and Administration)
1981:	Scholar-in-Residence: Rockefeller Foundation. Study Center, Bellagio, Italy
1984:	Information Technology Fellow: Edinburgh University, Scotland

CONSULTATIONS:

1960-1965:	Harvard University, Cambridge, MA (Building Planning)
	Fine Arts Library addition
	Francis A. Countway Library of Medicine
	Hilles Library, Radcliffe College
	Science Center Library
	Social Relations Library, William James Hall
1964:	M.I.T. Science Library, Cambridge, MA (Building Renovations)
1964:	University of Michigan, Health Science Information Center (Building)

1966:	Macalester College, St.Paul, MN (Building and Space)
1967:	Colby Junior College, New London, NH (Building and Space)
1967:	Museum of Fine Arts, Boston, MA (Building Planning)
1967:	Sarah Lawrence College, Bronxville, NY (Building and Space)
1968:	University Microfilms-Xerox (New Products)
1968:	Wesleyan University, Middletown, CT (Building and Automation)
1971:	Rice University, Houston, TX (Automation and Management)
1973:	Trinity College, Hartford, CT (Automation)
1974:	Holy Cross College, Worcester, MA (Building Planning)
1974:	Johns Hopkins University, Baltimore, MD (Automation)
1974:	M.I.T., Cambridge, MA (Automation)
1974:	University of Vermont, Burlington, VT (Instructional Technology)
1974:	3M Company, Minneapolis, MN (New Products)
1975:	Pahlavi National Library, Tehran, Iran (Building and Automation)
1975:	State University of New York, Stony Brook (Library Evaluation)
1976:	Keane College of New Jersey, Keane, NJ (Management)
1977:	American University, Washington, DC (Management)
1977:	Bell Telephone Laboratories, Murray Hill, NJ (Management and Technology)
1977:	Five Colleges, Inc., Amherst, MA (Library Cooperation)
1977:	University of Maine, Orono (Management)
1978:	Franklin and Marshall College, Lancaster, PA (Building and New Technology)
1978:	Miami University Library, Oxford, OH (Management)
1978:	State University of New York at Binghamton (Library Evaluation)
1978:	University of Guelph Library, Guelph, Ontario (Automation)
1978:	University of North Carolina, Chapel Hill (Building Planning)
1979:	Knowledge Industry Publications, Inc., White Plains, NY (Editorial Advisor)
1979:	MITRE Corporation, Metrek Division (Guide to Library Automation)
1979-1980:	KTO Press, Inc., Millwood, NY (Editorial Advisory Board)
1982:	New York Public Library The Research Libraries (Technology)
1982:	North Carolina State University (Technology and Space)
1983:	Johns Hopkins University, Washington, DC School of Advanced International Studies (Building Planning)
1983:	University of Iowa, Iowa City (Technology)
1983:	Virginia Polytechnic Institute, Blacksburg, VA (Evaluation of VTLS System)
1983:	Wheaton College, Norton, MA (Technology)
1983-1984:	New York Public Library The Research Libraries (Technology)
1985:	California State University, Long Beach, CA (Building and Technology)
1985:	Macalester College, St. Paul, MN (Building and Technology)
1985:	University of Iowa, Iowa City (Management)
1985:	University of Toronto, Toronto, Ont. (Management)
1986:	State University of New York, Stony Brook (Management)

1988:	The Getty Center for the History of Art and the Humanities, Los Angeles, CA (Management)
1992-1994:	Juma Al-Majid Center for Culture and Heritage, Dubai, U.A.E. (Building Planning)

EDITORIAL AND PUBLICATION BOARDS:

1969-1970:	Chemical Abstracts Service: Advisory Board
1969-1972:	College and Research Libraries: Editorial Board
1973-1978:	Journal of Library Automation: Editorial Board
1976-:	Social Science Citation Index: Advisory Board
1977-1979:	Information Science Abstracts: Board of Directors
1978-:	Outline for Research Libraries: Editorial Advisory Board
1982-:	Interlending and Document Supply: Honorary Editor
1983-1987:	BLLD Review (British Lending Library Division): Editorial Board
1987-:	Library Hi Tech: Editorial Board

LIBRARY VISITING COMMITTEES:

1973-1986:	Harvard University, Overseers Committee to Visit the Library
1975-1977:	Brown University Library
1977:	University of Virginia, Library
1978-1984:	M.I.T. Overseers Committee on the Library
1982:	Emory University Library
1982-1988:	Johns Hopkins University Library
1983:	New York University Library
1992-:	Georgetown University Library Advisory Committee

HONORS AND AWARDS:

1971:	Council on Library Resources Fellowship to attend the Advanced Management Program at the Harvard Business School
1975:	Purdue University Library Centennial Lecture
1977:	First Place Winner, American Libraries Prize Article Competition
1979:	R.R. Bowker Memorial Lecturer
1980:	University of Tennessee Library Lecturer
1981:	Keynote Speaker: Joint Conference of AAL/NZLA Christchurch, NZ, followed by a lecture tour in Australia
1983:	Samuel Lazerow Memorial Lecturer
1986:	Melvil Dewey Medal
1986:	Keynote Speaker: Second National Conference on Online Public Access to Library Files, University of Bath, Centre for Catalogue Research.
1988:	Keynote Speaker: US-USSR Seminar on Access to Library Resources through Technology and Preservation, Washington, DC.
1989:	Distinguished Alumnus Award, Columbia University School of Library Service
1989:	Festschrift in honor of Richard DeGennaro based on the proceedings of the 12th International Essen Symposium under the title, "Developments in Microcomputing: Discovering New Opportunities for Libraries in the 1990s."
1991:	Honorary Doctor of Humane Letters, Wabash College
1991:	Distinguished Alumnus Award, Wesleyan University
1991:	Academic or Research Librarian of the Year Award, Association of College and Research Libraries
1993:	Hugh C. Atkinson Memorial Award, American Library Association

CLUBS:

1979-1987:	Franklin Inn Club, Philadelphia, PA
1987-:	Grolier Club, New York
1987-:	Harvard Club of New York
1988-:	Century Association, New York

Compiled by Carol Ishimoto
January, 1996, Harvard College Library.

DE GENNARO
SELECTED BIBLIOGRAPHY

Libraries, Technology, and the Information Marketplace: Selected Papers, by Richard De Gennaro. Boston, G.K.Hall, 1987. 432p.

This collection is divided in two parts. The first part contains six essays that explore current perspectives on the subjects covered in the second part. The thirty-three articles and essays in the second part cover a twenty-year period of unparalleled development in libraries, library networks, and the publishing and information industries.

PART I: THE FUTURE IN PERSPECTIVE

The following six essays were published in this volume for the first time:

> "Surviving Technological Revolutions,"(1987): 3-5.
> "Technology and Access," (1987): 7-11.
> "Libraries in the Marketplace," (1987): 13-17.
> "Online Catalogs and Integrated Systems," (1987): 19-29.
> "Electronic Data Files: the New Frontier," (1987): 31-35.
> "Libraries and Computing Centers in the Wired University," (1987): 37-41.

PART II: ESSAYS AND PAPERS

The following thirty-three essays have been previously published and are arranged in reverse chronological order within the following four categories: Libraries and the Information Marketplace; Managing the Library in Transition; Library Technology and Networking; and, Library Automation: the Early Years.

(1) *LIBRARIES AND THE INFORMATION MARKETPLACE*

"Libraries, Technology, and the Information Marketplace," *Library Journal* (1 June 1982): 1045-1054. This paper was written during a residency at the Villa Serboloni, the Rockefeller Foundation's Study Center in Bellagio, Italy in the Spring of 1981. It was presented at Wesleyan University's Sesquicentennial Symposium, "Knowledge in an Information Era." Also reprinted in: *Library Lit. 13 - The Best of 1982*, edited by Bill Katz (Metuchen, N.J., Scarecrow Press, 1983); *National Forum: Phi Beta Kappa Journal*, Summer 1983. Also published in Danish in: *Bibliotek 70*, Bibliotekarforbundets blad 1982-15.

"Research Libraries Enter the Information Age," *Library Journal* (15 November 1979): 1205-1210. Also published in the R.R. Bowker Lecture series, 1980; reprinted in *Library Lit. 10 - The Best of 1979.*

"Copyright, Resource Sharing, and Hard Times: a View from the Field," *American Libraries* (September 1977): 430-435. First place winner in round 2 of the *American Libraries*' Prize Article Competition. Also reprinted in: *Technology and*

Copyright, edited by G.P. Bush and R.H. Dreyfuss (Mt. Airy, MD: Lomond Books, 1979); *The Copyright Dilemma*, edited by H.S. White (Chicago, ALA, 1978)

"Escalating Journal Prices: Time to Fight Back," *American Libraries* (February 1977): 69-74. Also reprinted in: *Library Lit. 8 - The Best of 1977.*

"Pay Libraries and User Charges," *Library Journal* (February 15, 1975): 363-367.

"Providing Bibliographic Services from Machine-Readable Data Bases: the Library's Role," *Journal of Library Automation* 6, no.4 (December 1973): 215-222.

(2) *MANAGING THE LIBRARY IN TRANSITION*

"Shifting Gears: Information Technology and the Academic Library," *Library Journal* (June 15, 1984): 1204-1209. The paper was presented at the School of Library and Information Science, University of Pittsburgh in 1983 as the Samuel Lazerow Memorial Lecture. Also reprinted in *Libraries and Information Science in the Electronic Age*, edited by Hendrik Edelman. (Philadelphia, ISI Press, 1986).

"Theory vs. Practice in Library Management," *Library Journal* (July 1983): 1318-1321.

"Matching Commitments to Needs and Resources," *Journal of Academic Librarianship* (March 1981): 9-13. This paper was given initially as the University of Tennessee Library Lecture in 1980 and published in Library Lectures, University of Tennessee, Knoxville, 1981.

"Library Statistics and User Satisfaction: No Significant Correlation," *Journal of Academic Librarianship (May* 1980): 95.

"Library Administration and New Management Systems," *Library Journal* (December 15, 1978): 2477-2482. Also reprinted in: *Library Lit. 10 - The Best of 1979; Strategies for Library Administration*, edited by C.R. McClure and A.R. Samuels (Littleton, CO, Libraries Unlimited, 1982); *Management Strategies for Libraries, a Basic Reader*, edited by Beverly P. Lynch (New York, Neal-Schuman, 1985)

"The Changing Fortunes of Research Libraries: a Response to "Pitt and the Pendulum"," *Library Journal* (February 1, 1978): 320-321.

"Impact on On-Line Services on the Academic Library." In: *Online Revolution in Libraries;* proceedings of the 1977 Conference in Pittsburgh, PA, edited by Allen Kent and Thomas J. Galvin (New York, Dekker, 1978):177-181.

"Austerity, Technology, and Resource Sharing: Research Libraries Face the Future," *Library Journal* (May 15, 1975): 917-923. Also reprinted in: *Library Lit. 6 - The Best of 1975*, edited by Bill Katz (Metuchen, N.J., Scarecrow Press, 1976)

"Less is more: the University of Pennsylvania Reorganizes its Library Support for Regional Studies." In: *South Asian Library Resources in North America;* papers from the Boston Conference, 1974, edited by M.L.P. Patterson and M. Yanuck (Zug, Switzerland, Inter Documentation Co., 1975)

(3) *LIBRARY TECHNOLOGY AND NETWORKING*

"Integrated Online Library Systems: Perspectives, Perceptions, and Practicalities," *Library Journal* (February 1, 1985): 37-40. A version of this paper was presented at the

Second Conference on Integrated Online Library Systems held in Atlanta, Georgia in September 1984 and published by Genaway & Associates in 1985.

"Will Success Spoil OCLC?" *Library Journal* (April 1, 1984):626.

"Library Automation and Networking: Perspectives on Three Decades," *Library Journal* (April 1, 1983): 629-635.   A version of this paper was presented at the 1982 Essen Symposium: Increasing Productivity through Library Automation, Essen, Germany. An abridged version in Swedish was published in *Bibliotekariesamfundet Meddelar 2* (1984). A Spanish translation was published in *Notas Bibliotecologicas* by the Biblioteca Benjamin Franklin in Mexico City, 1985.

"Libraries and Networks in Transition: Problems and Prospects for the 1980"s," *Library Journal* (March 15, 1981): 1045-1049.   A version of this paper was given initially as the keynote address at the LAA/NZLA Conference, Christchurch, N.Z., January 19, 1981.

"Computer Network Systems: the Impact of Technology on   Co-operative Interlending in the U.S.A.," *Interlending Review* 9 (April 1981): 39-43. This is a revised version of a paper presented at the International Seminar on National Document Provision, Boston Spa, England, September 22-24, 1980.

"Resource Sharing in a Network Environment," *Library Journal* (February 1, 1980): 353-355.

"From Monopoly to Competition: the Changing Library Network Scene," *Library Journal* (June 1, 1979): 1215-1217.

"The Role of the Academic Library in Networking." In: *Networks for Networkers*; proceedings of the Conference on Networks for Networkers, Indianapolis, 1979, edited by B.E. Markuson and B. Woolls (New York, Neal-Schuman, 1980): 304-308.

"Doing Business with Vendors in the Computer-Based Library Systems Marketplace," *American Libraries* (April 1978):212,221-222.

"Wanted: a Minicomputer Serials Control System," *Library Journal* (April 15, 1977): 878-879.

"Library Automation: Changing Patterns and New Directions," *Library Journal* (January, 1, 1976): 175-183.   Also reprinted in: *Reference and Information Services: A Reader*, edited by Bill Katz and Andrea Tarr (Metuchen, N.J., Scarecrow Press, 1978)

"Library Automation: the Second Decade," *Journal of Library Automation* 8 (March 1975): 3-4.

(4) *LIBRARY AUTOMATION: THE EARLY YEARS*

"A National Bibliographic Data Base in Machine-Readable Form: Progress and Prospects," *Library Trends* 18 (April 1970):537-550.

"Harvard University's Widener Library Shelflist Conversion and Publication Program," *College and Research Libraries* (September 1970): 318-331.   Also reprinted in: *Book Catalogs*, edited by M. Tauber and H. Feinberg (Metuchen, N.J., Scarecrow Press, 1971)

"The Development and Administration of Automated Systems in Academic Libraries," *Journal of Library Automation* 1, no.1 (March 1968): 75-90.   This was the lead

paper in the first issue of the *Journal of Library Automation*. It was one of the first
major papers on the organization and management of library automation and was
well-received and widely cited. Also reprinted in: *Key Papers in Information
Science* (Washington, D.C., ASIS, 1971)

"Automation in the Harvard College Library," *Harvard Library Bulletin* 16, no.3 (July
1968): 217-236.

"A Strategy for the Conversion of Research Library Catalogs to Machine Readable Form,"
College and Research Libraries (July 1967): 253-257.

"A Computer Produced Shelf List," College and Research Libraries (July 1965): 311-
315,353. This was the author's first published article which described one of the
first library shelflist conversion projects.

In addition to the thirty-nine essays and papers included above, the author has published another
twenty papers and given a number of presentations at conferences and seminars, the proceedings of
which were not always published. The following titles, arranged in chronological order, have been
selected as examples of the author's opinion papers which had their impact on the library profession
and the information industry.

"Participative Management or Unionization?" College and Research Libraries (May 1972):
173-174.

"Resource Sharing for Libraries: Major Trends in Library Computerization." In: Facts and
Futures: What's Happening Now in Computing for Higher Education. Proceedings
of the EDUCOM Fall Conference, October 9, 10, 11, 1973, Princeton, NJ.
(Princeton, NJ, EDUCOM, c1974): 282-286.

"Public Notice: We, the Librarians, Are No Longer Responsible for the Debts of Our
Former Suitors," American Libraries (September 1975): 456-457.

"Major Research Library and the New Copyright Act [with discussion]. In: Copyright
Dilemma (ALA, 1978): 147-162.

"From Growth to Change, From Acquisitions to Access: the Research Library of the
Future." *Library Issues,* 3, no.4, 1983. Paper presented at the Wingspread
Conference: Toward the 21st Century, a Conference on Research Libraries and
Their Users, Dec. 8-10, 1982.

"The Online Catalog and Beyond: a North American Perspective." In: *Online Public Access
to Library Files.* Second   National Conference [1986, University of Bath,
Centre for Catalogue Research] Janet Kinsella, Editor. (Oxford, Eng., Elsevier
International Bulletin, c1986): 5-16. Keynote address.

"Toward a Network of Networks: Trends and Issues in U.S. Library Automation."
Unpublished paper delivered at the symposium, *U.S. and Japanese Libraries in
Higher Education: the Binational Experience,* Tokyo, August 24, 1986.

"The Automation of Libraries and Information Services in the United States." In:
*Proceedings of the US-USSR Seminar on Access to Library Resources through
Technology and Preservation,* Washington, DC, July 5-8, 1988. (Each paper is
separately paged.) Keynote speaker. January, 1996